ADVANCE I

"An excellent practical guide to living your authentic self. Highly recommended."

Richard Barrett, Chairman of the Barrett Values Centre

"*my31Practices* is an eminently practical blueprint that will help you craft the life you want to live and experience."

Srikumar Rao, CEO, The Rao Institute
(also known as The Happiness Guru)

"In this complex and challenging world, having a core set of personal values which help guide your decisions and actions can be hugely powerful. But where do you start? This book walks you through the key considerations in defining your values and the everyday practices which will help you stay true to them. It draws on a broad spectrum of psychological theories and summarises them neatly in a concise and actionable manner. A potentially life-defining read."

Steve Apps, Chair, Association for Business Psychology

"This book is very special for me to read as it captures many elements of the approach I have developed over 25 years as a coach for business leaders. The way in which comprehensive reference literature and different methods are brought together to support the my31Practices approach in such a logical, practical, and easy to follow way is truly impressive."

Tore Palmén, Founder, Values Academy, Sweden

"*My 31 Practices* is a very practical guide, which shows you a step by step way to gain peace and meaningfulness in your life as well as how to successfully heal the stresses in life. A methodology and lots of great tips you can use immediately! Bravo!"

Shelle Rose Charvet, author of *Words That Change Minds*

"Alan and Steve build on the excellent 31Practices book with new thinking drawn from positive psychology and neuroscience which challenges our thinking about who we are and what we do. They successfully blend together science, story-telling, and practice and have produced another great read."

Professor Jonathan Passmore, University of Evora, Portugal

"The structure, straightforward composition, and easy to follow implementation of the methodology in this book are unparalleled in an industry often rife with good intentions and poor execution."

Stephen Doran, author of *Burn the Bullshit*

"With achievable steps, this book invites all of us to live and practice our core values in daily life, to make small differences with a massive impact. A special recommendation for parents and teachers: *My 31 Practices* is an excellent manual to practice and teach the language of values to children and adolescents."

Patrik Somers Stephenson, co-editor, *A World Book of Values*

"I am not generally a fan of self-development books, but this one is different. The book provides a route map with step by step guidance and practical examples for people to regain control of self, to be consciously authentic both in work and in social life – to be the Real You."

Ricky Qin, Strengths Coach and Talent Development Consultant, Shanghai, China

"Our Minessence mantra is 'Making a significant contribution to having everyone in society able to live a meaningful life.' This book makes a valuable contribution by helping people in the process of unfolding meaning through values."

Paul Chippendale, Founding Director, Minessence International Cooperative Ltd

"If you are self-aware, self-disciplined, and committed to making positive changes in your life, this book holds many keys!"

Patrick Sweeney, Co-Author of The New York Times Bestseller, *Succeed on Your Own Terms*

"My 31 Practices is a powerful book which enables you to improve your life, through increased alignment and performance, together with greater confidence and fulfilment. Individuals have to create value for themselves and values is the way to start. This book shows you how – human sense makes business sense."

Gautam Mahajan, Founder editor, *Journal of Creating Value*

"Rich with insight, extensively referenced, and encouragingly readable, this book explores the landscape of consciously values based living with great enthusiasm. There can be no doubt that at this point in time there is a need for us, both individually and collectively, to find new ways of framing and tackling the issues of the day – my31Practices can help us do just that."

Jackie Le Fèvre, Director, Magma Effect

"my31Practices is a values-based approach to help you lead the life you want to be living. It holds your hand as it takes you through a process that really will transform the results you get in your life."

Simon Horton, Author of *The Leader's Guide to Negotiation: How to use soft skills to get hard results*, published by the Financial Times

"Alan Williams and Steve Payne have provided a wonderfully pragmatic guide for helping you release the power of your values. In our massively accelerating world, we need new ways of embracing change and new tools to make the most of our lives. my31Practices can help!"

Grant Soosalu, Co-developer of the new field of multiple Brain Integration Techniques (mBIT)

"Research confirms the importance of knowing and living by your own personal values, and my31Practices is an excellent way of turning your values into behaviours and developing these behaviours into habits. I highly recommend this accessible and inspirational book to anyone who is seeking a springboard to a greater sense of well-being and making a difference to others through the way you live your life."

Dr Ruth Mann, Head of Evidence, National Offender Management Service

"Alan and Steve's book, drawing on a wide range of material from story, NLP, and Mindfulness, enables the reader to experience 'what is on the tin' – deep and lasting personal and professional change and enhancement. Well done Alan and Steve for crafting something that works."

Robbie Steinhouse, author of *How to Coach with NLP*

We dedicate this book to each and every
person who is on the journey to discover
their VALUES Superhero and, in particular,
to those who are making the first step.

In loving memory of Mary Payne
(August 5th 1939 – July 28th 2016) who
listened, guided, fought, loved and protected
– a VALUES Superhero *passing through
nature to eternity.*

Published by
LID Publishing Ltd.
One Adam Street, London. WC2N 6LE

31 West 34th Street, 8th Floor, Suite 8004
New York, NY 10001, US

info@lidpublishing.com
www.lidpublishing.com

A member of:

BPR
Business Publishers Roundtable

www.businesspublishersroundtable.com

Printed in Great Britain by TJ International
ISBN: 978-1-910649-87-9

my

31

Practices

Release the power of your values
for authentic happiness

LONDON   MONTERREY
MADRID   SHANGHAI
MEXICO CITY   BOGOTA
NEW YORK   BUENOS AIRES
BARCELONA   SAN FRANCISCO

CONTENTS

FOREWORD

Alan Williams and Steve Payne have succeeded in elevating this book to a position of easy accessibility. This work is certainly not the ordinary self-help manual. Rather, it translates individual values into behaviour, and every step of the journey is supported by empirical evidence. Using a neuro-linguistic programming (NLP) lens, the authors emphasize the importance of physiological and psychological synthesis which begins with one's identification of his or her most salient values and beliefs. The authors certainly do not postulate a one-size-fits-all approach, but stress the importance of self-examination, societal interaction, and deliberative thinking. Even after values are delineated, there is no Presidential-like charge to action. Rather, a period of assessment and reflection must occur first and empathy for others exercised. The reader is asked to predict the consequences of implementing his or her views in society and be ready to realign and adjust them if deleterious results are deemed inevitable. After looking inward, the individual must project forward, accepting constructive feedback in the process. This journey stimulates self-reflection and situational critique and uses one's values as a basis for moulding actionable behaviours. The authors realize that their model must be malleable to accommodate a person's unique situation and environment and further promote the objectives of happiness and efficacy of one's life and purpose.

This book is a call to action and to avoid complacency with the status quo. It emphasizes *being* over *doing* and aids the individual to define his or her core values to form a moral compass as well as incorporate self-discipline. There are repeated, and necessary, admonitions to stop, reflect, assess, and adjust wherever necessary. The quests to experience life's opportunities and challenges and to act outside of one's comfort zone are heralded over materialism. Signposting to a plethora of videos and other resources are integrated throughout the chapters to guide the reader to embrace a habit of making skilful and non-judgmental choices while appreciating the similarities of all people through affirmative conduct and conversation. No individual should cower from new experiences since, as the authors opine, we are all lifelong learners and have access to many different ways to acquire new knowledge. The authors further encourage the reader to experience, analyze, and ultimately, implement and underscore the following tenets:

- Practice breeds confidence.
- Performance leads to improvement.
- Positive reinforcement allows for healthier individual growth.
- Mistakes are learning tools.

Finally, *My 31 Practices* demonstrates the need to respect others while embarking upon this journey of self-discovery.

Elizabeth F. R. Gingerich. J.D.
Journal of Values-Based Leadership, Editor-in-Chief

ACKNOWLEDGEMENTS

Where to start? There have been so many amazing, talented people who we have had the privilege to connect and collaborate with during this book project. Perhaps it is because we are operating in the values space that we have found a general mind set of helpfulness, generosity and encouragement. For this reason, there are too many people to mention individually by name but we want to recognise you all for your contribution.

We have received positive feedback about our book from colleagues from all over the world. It has been particularly fulfilling to receive feedback from people from different walks of life, but who have all connected with the my31Practices approach for one reason or another.

In Part Four of the book, you will see that we have included stories from people who have used the my31Practices approach. These stories were chosen from those submitted by a larger group of people who volunteered to give my31Practices a try. We thank everyone for their open mindedness and willingness to explore something new.

We are in admiration of the many experts whose work we have drawn on to develop, challenge and support our thinking, and found inspiration from the creators of the quotes we have used to reinforce key messages. So many people have helped craft the final version of the book, from design experts to random people we have met in the street (literally) and of course family and friends. It has been great working with the LID Publishing team again and we are grateful to the way in which the British Library, various bars and coffee shops, Dropbox and Skype have all helped us work together to make this book possible.

Finally, a special thank you to Alison Whybrow, co-author of the first book, *The 31 Practices*, about how the 31Practices approach applies at an organizational level. Alison provided great expertise and insight from a psychology perspective in helping to articulate why the 31Practices approach is so successful, and the book has received international acclaim.

This second book embraces everything from the first book, and is focused on how the 31Practices approach applies at an individual, personal level. In other ways, however, it is very different in style, designed more as an "action book" and providing a whole new layer of insight with a neuro-linguistic programming (NLP) perspective.

We are very proud to be connected with all of you and thank you sincerely for your interest, time and spirit to collaborate.

PART 1

INTRODUCTION

The first part of the book provides a general background and context to the my31Practices approach and the book. Here in Chapter 1, we lay out the book's structure and contents to help you decide how you want to go about reading it – in your own way. Then, the next three chapters deal with the why, how and what: Chapter 2 *Why* provides an overview of why the my31Practices approach is so valuable, Chapter 3 *How* explains how the approach works at a conceptual and theoretical level, and Chapter 4 *What* gives an overview of what you do at a practical level. Finally, Chapter 5 *Template* provides an example set of myValues, myPractices, and myExperiences so you can see what you will be able to create for yourself by using the my31Practices approach. These chapters are an introduction ahead of a deeper exploration of the underpinnings and how my31Practices works, covered in Part 2.

GUIDE

PART 1   INTRODUCTION

PURPOSE

FIND YOUR

CORE VALUES

BEING VS DOING

PART 2

my 31 Practices

PART 3

NLP

STORIES

PART 4

PART 5

RECAP

JOURNEY

PART 6

"It is our choices, Harry, that show what we truly are,
far more than our abilities."
J K Rowling, Dumbledore, in Harry Potter
and the Chamber of Secrets[i]

Welcome and thank you for choosing to read our book. You might be surprised to learn that we believe the value of self-help and self-improvement books is generally overstated. Furthermore, the credentials of these authors are uneven, and research has documented the general absence of empirical evidence supporting the advice which is so freely made available in amazingly large volumes[ii] (sorry for the pun!).

In our opinion, it is not the "content" of these books that makes a difference but, instead, the application and action by the reader, in their own "context" – what a difference just one letter makes! This practical book can help you to be power*ful* if you choose to take action using the tools and techniques offered, but the book itself is power*less*. Our best hope is it will inspire you to do something different, however small, and that you will notice a positive impact or shift, either on yourself or on the people around you – or both. Our intention is that this book will help you to connect with, explore, understand, and be the best version of you and that it will help your behaviour to be aligned with what is important to you – in other words for you to become congruent. We describe this as discovering, or at least seeing a glimpse of, your unique VALUES Superhero, which is present in each of us. In this way, you can release the power of your values for authentic happiness.

We draw on many sources of empirical evidence throughout this book, but, as we are discovering every day, all that we know (or imagine) has not yet been proven. In this book, we are very comfortable drawing on the tangible experience of respected experts as well as our own thoughts, ideas and personal experiences in addition to published research. We trust that you will find this to be an interesting, thought provoking, stimulating and even inspiring combination.

> *"We tend to overvalue the things we can measure and undervalue the things we cannot."*
> *John Hayes[iii]*

This book builds on the approach developed in the first book, *The 31 Practices*.[iv] Why wouldn't we do this when it received such critical acclaim internationally? One of our favourite endorsements highlighted the elements of simplicity, holistic approach and robust underpinnings:

Lesley Kuhn, senior lecturer and professor at the School of Business, University of Western Sydney, said: "What stands out for me in 31Practices is the elegance of the 360 degree facilitated integration – with the approach well supported by a range of seriously impressive research."

Already, the my31Practices approach for individuals is receiving recognition from highly respected sources. Dr Sally Vanson, master trainer of NLP, behavioural change consultant and visiting university professor/fellow says: "The my31Practices approach of self-reflection and action gives us a methodology to pause, to stop and think about our desires for the standard of our personal lives and professional work, and how to align this with our holistic well-being, giving us new found confidence to support our clients, colleagues, families, and of course ourselves, in our challenges."

We have designed the book to be engaging and interactive beyond the written word. Each chapter is introduced by an illustration for you to add your own finishing touches or even colour in. We have also selected inspirational quotes in support of our key messages and trust you will find these a helpful and enjoyable addition.

> *"In theory, there is no difference between theory*
> *and practice. In practice, there is."*
> *Yogi Berra[v]*

GLOSSARY

Throughout the book you will notice reference to particular terms making up a mini my31Practices vocabulary. Here is a quick translation guide:

31Practices: the name of the overall approach applied to organizations; helping to translate their stated values into employees' daily behaviour.

my31Practices: the name of the overall approach applied to individuals; helping you to translate your personal values into daily behaviour.

myValues: the set of five personal values you identify as being most important to you; your essence. The way to identify these is covered in Chapter 6 *Values*, and Chapter 20 *Beliefs*.

myPractices: your set of 31 practical day-to-day behaviours created from your myValues. The way to make these really effective is covered in Chapter 8 *Metaphor* and Chapter 9 *Affirmation*.

myExperiences: your record of what happened with your myPractice for the day and what the impact was on you and other people around you. You will read about the benefit of doing this in many of the chapters in Part 2 and Part 3.

www.my31Practices.com: the mobile-friendly website where you can capture your myValues, myPractices and myExperiences.

myHub: your "homepage" at www.my31Practices.com where you can access all of the information about your my31Practices.

VALUES Superhero: the best version of yourself. We can all connect with and release the power of our own VALUES Superhero. The my31Practices approach helps you to do this.

In addition, we have made a conscious decision to use the American spelling of the word "practice" for both the noun and the verb in the interest of uniformity and flow.

PART 1
- Introduction

Why would you choose to read any part of this book? You are busy and have a hundred and one other things you could be doing. We understand this. This is the reason why we have carefully designed the book as a quick, easy read.

With its very practical style, this book can be dipped into, by section, by chapter, or even by any of the suggested activities, which encourages you to think and, more importantly, do something different – think of it as an 'action book'. If you have more time, you can read the book from cover to cover. Whatever way you choose, we want you to enjoy the experience rather than to think of it as a chore. Whether you are interested in values already, just curious, or a sceptic, any of these is fine. You also have different moods on different days, different preferences and choices. In summary, our book is not designed for the mass market. It is written for you to make it what you want it to be, to enjoy as and when you choose.

The first part of the book provides a general background and context to the my31Practices approach. Here in Chapter 1 *Guide*, we lay out the structure and contents of the book to help you decide how you want to go about reading it – in your own way. The next three chapters deal with the why, how and what: Chapter 2 *Why* provides an overview of why the my31Practices approach is so valuable, Chapter 3 *How* explains the approach at a conceptual and theoretical level, and Chapter 4 *What* gives an overview at a practical level. Chapter 5 *Template* provides an example set of myValues, myPractices, and myExperiences so you can see what you will be able to create yourself by using the my31Practices approach. These chapters are an introduction ahead of a deeper exploration of the underpinnings and how my31Practices works, covered in Part 2.

PART 2
– Underpinnings

This part of the book explores the various features and thinking of the my31Practices approach. Chapter 6 *Values* introduces this fundamental topic in general terms; Chapter 7 *Mindfulness* explores the relevance of "being present"'; Chapter 8 *Metaphor* deals with the power of creative thinking; Chapter 9 *Affirmation* covers the importance of mindset and vocabulary; Chapter 10 *Learning* gives an overview of how you take in new things; Chapter 11 *Habit* is focused on how behaviour is embedded; Chapter 12 *Practice* deals with the topic of repeated action for high performance; Chapter 13 *Reinforcement* details methods to encourage repeated behaviour; and Chapter 14 *Assessment* considers the role of understanding what has been achieved. All of the chapters explain how these individual topics support and reinforce the my31Practices approach. Some chapters are long, some short, there is not a standard approach to the length; just what felt "right" for each topic. Many of the chapters mention additional resources to explore, such as reference notes to read, activities to try, and each chapter leaves you with a QR code if you want to know more and leaves you with a thought-provoking question. This is intended to stimulate exploration, discovery, feeling, thinking and action. We want the book to be more than just words, and to help inspire you beyond its covers.

PART 3
- NLP

Part 3 is an exploration of the practical elements of my31Practices and provides some useful information, tools and strategies to help you create and implement your myPractices. This section also explains why it all works, through a neuro-linguistic programming (NLP) lens. Its purpose is to enable you to develop your insight into how and why the my31Practices approach works from a human perspective. We explore a number of topics and continue with additional exercises and signposting to further resources. Part 3 is designed to support Part 2, but it isn't essential to have read it to work with my31Practices in your daily life.

We have organized this section into the following chapters: Chapter 15 *NLP* is a summary exploration of the NLP approach; Chapter 16 *Maps* demonstrates how we create our versions of reality; Chapter 17 *Presuppositions* explores the concept of assumed truths and their impact; Chapter 18 *Awareness* shares how we can become more aware of ourselves and others; Chapter 19 *Alignment* looks at a process for making sure our choices are aligned; Chapter 20 *Beliefs* examines the importance and impact of beliefs on performance; Chapter 21 *mBIT* highlights an entirely new field in NLP coaching that aligns head, heart and gut; and Chapter 22 *Goals* looks at some simple, yet powerful, processes for successful goal setting. However, you will notice a lot of overlap and connection between these chapters because many of them are part of each other. We suggest that you read chapters 15 *NLP* and 16 *Maps* first and then feel free to start with a subject that you are most attracted to and follow your interests from there.

PART 4
- Stories

This part of the book provides an insight into people's experiences of using the my31Practices approach. The stories in Chapters 23–28 might touch on topics, thoughts and feelings that you have: hopes, aspirations, questions, concerns and reservations. We start with a perspective from a professional who uses values as a basis for her personal coaching business in Chapter 23 *Coach*. Then we have five personal stories from co-author Alan Williams in Chapter 24 *Practitioner*, followed by Chapter 25 *Traveller*, Chapter

26 *Firestarter*, Chapter 27 *Changemaker*, and Chapter 28 *Seeker*. We are very grateful to everybody who submitted their personal perspectives of using the my31Practices approach. We trust that you will find the stories we have chosen to be an interesting collection written by real people around the world from very different walks of life.

PART 5
- Recap

If you are super-busy, with no time to read even this short, quick read action book, we offer a summary in Chapter 29 *Recap*.

PART 6
- Journey

With this part of the book, we have followed the style of a number of more recent films and novels where the beginning is not at the beginning. Part 6 is a prequel that shares the 31Practices journey from the beginning, to provide a deeper insight into the background and development of the approach, as well as taking a look at developments and possibilities for 31Practices and my31Practices. Chapter 30 *Beginning* deals with the origination and evolution of the 31Practices approach and how the first *The 31 Practices* book came to be published, while Chapter 31 *Present* considers the current and emerging agenda, with a look at what might be possible in the future.

To end the book, there is a quiz about everything you have read. No prizes for guessing how many questions there are!

TO FINISH

Several people have voiced a common frustration that in the self-improvement and self-help industry, many books are promoted as a sure-fire formula for success and fulfilment, because the approach outlined worked for the author. If this is true, we have the following questions:[vi]

- Why is the industry worth $11billion and still growing?
- Why is it the biggest genre of books sold?
- Why are 80% of self-improvement/self-help book buyers repeat purchasers?

Each individual's development and growth is a process of interaction with, and adaptation to, their own unique environment and context – which is why this won't be the last personal development book. People who have used the methodology tell us that my31Practices offers a highly effective framework which helps to translate personal values into a set of very practical day-to-day behaviours and then provides the discipline and structure to practice these behaviours in life in a sustainable way. We trust that our book will inspire people, one person at a time, to find something helpful and valuable, however small, in the my31Practices approach and, more importantly, to do something about it. Ultimately, the more you put in, the more you get out. How valuable is authentic happiness to you?

PAUSE FOR THOUGHT ...

What choices will you make about how to go about reading this book?

WANT TO KNOW MORE?

http://www.my31practices.com/the-book/resources/chapter-1

WHY

DO YOU WANT TO BE...

"Be a first-rate version of yourself, not a second rate-version of someone else."
Judy Garland[i]

Do you want to be more comfortable with who you are and feel less stressed? Do you want to be the best version of you? Do you want to be happy? For most of us, "Yes" is an easy answer to these questions, but to achieve authentic happiness in practice is more of a challenge.

From the beginning of civilization – and maybe before – people have looked for guidance to lead their lives as a good person. Sources are as old as the Ten Commandments in the Holy Bible or similar references in the Koran or in Buddhism. You might be surprised to know that there is also more than one version of the Native American Indian ten commandments.[ii]

In the past 2,000 years, there has been an astonishing amount of change, and life has become more hectic and complex. We have become much richer financially, but we have also created the phrase "time poor". Despite our increase in material wealth, and our busyness "doing", we are no happier now than we were 50 years ago. Professor Richard Layard calls this the "hedonic treadmill".[iii] Because of the constant demands on us, there is less time to reflect, to consider, and to question whether we are behaving the right way. Our time is totally consumed with "doing" what we need to do.

There are many reasons for this; we have listed a few, but you might well want to add some others. There has been rapid technological, social and economic change. We are overloaded with information, and fear for our financial and job security, so the hedonic treadmill has become all-consuming. Some people turn to alcohol, smoking, drugs, food, or shopping as a short-term "fix"– but these can cause more stress and even ill health.

At the same time, community infrastructure has changed, arguably becoming weaker, and the traditional concept of family has evolved into something less certain and more diverse. Greater numbers of people face increasing pressures with less family and community support. There is a widespread focus on material wealth, but this does not increase happiness after we reach a certain level of income.

We live in an age of stress. A report[iv] from the Mental Health Foundation indicates that societies are increasingly fearful and anxious, backing the latest statistics that show a long-term increase in the rate of anxiety disorders. As an example, depression, anxiety and stress are the cause of about ten million lost working days per year in the UK alone.[v] The effects of this social fragmentation appear to be recognized by the general public – a study by Opinium Research[vi] found that:

- 81% of people agree that "the fast pace of life and the number of things we have to do and worry about these days is a major cause of stress, unhappiness and illness".
- 86% of people agree that "people would be much happier and healthier if they knew how to slow down and live in the moment".

Tiger Woods is one of the most high-profile examples in recent years of what these circumstances can lead to[vii] and, in his words, "I had gotten away from my core values".[viii]

And yet this may not be a totally modern phenomenon, as some would have you believe. Having read the above, you would not be surprised to see these quotes:

"What are you looking at? To what goal are you straining? The whole future lies in uncertainty: live immediately."[ix]

"The evil springs not from persisting without elasticity in what one has attempted, but from originally attempting too much, from filling one's programme till it runs over. The only cure is to reconstitute the programme, and to attempt less."[x]

What may be more of a surprise is to learn that the first quote is from Lucius Annaeus Seneca,[xi] written 2,000 years ago and the second was from Enoch Arnold Bennett[xii] in 1920. Finding authentic happiness is the eternal human quest (see Chapter 19 *Alignment*).

BEING VS DOING

So, do you find that you are endlessly busy at work and in your social life? Is this the case some of the time, if not all of the time? If you recognize this, it should not surprise you. It is very easy to be busy "doing" without much thought about how you are behaving – swept along on a current of 'busyness' rather than making more conscious decisions. Soon you can be caught in thinking habits that are at best unsustainable, and, at worst, are destructive. Under this pressure, you can feel out of control and lose touch with your personal core values, your core purpose, and what creates meaning for you – just like Tiger.

This "doing" mode fundamentally enables you to live and to achieve your goals. But it doesn't help you thrive emotionally – or be in touch with yourself, other people, or the world you live in. Jon Kabat-Zinn[xiii] notes that by staying in "doing" mode, we are in danger of "dying without actually fully living". What is it that you are doing and why are you doing it? What choices are you making in the way you live? After all, you are a human "being" not a human "doing".

Of course you can't stop "doing" altogether. You need to get things done and make decisions to live. But you can also practice being present and more aware in the here and now of what is happening around you. When was the last time that you asked yourself "why am I doing this?" and thought beyond reflex answers such as "it's part of my job" or "my partner asked me to"? Have you gone even further to ask "what is this all for?" When have you taken the time to step back and really consider this question, and perhaps even done something to live in a way that is more aligned with who you are?

If you don't "know" who you are, and are not aware of the way that you are "being", then what you *do* is mind-*less* rather than mind*ful*. At best, your doing is aligned by chance to your purpose and values, and at worst, it is totally disconnected.

Imagine how it would be if, in your "doing mode", your actions and behaviours were expressions of your core purpose and values. The my31Practices version of "being" involves a consciously-shaped awareness of what is important to you and designing your own personal compass to guide your day-to-day behaviour. How comfortable are you that you are leading the life you want; that you are "being" the person you want to be; that your thoughts, feelings, words and actions are aligned; that you are being the best version of yourself?

How can you learn to align yourself? How can you display strong self-leadership? How can you release the power of your VALUES Superhero? How can you do this starting today?

"We can be heroes, just for one day."
David Bowie[xiv]

ANOTHER WAY

There is another way. How many people do you know who invest time, effort and money in going to the gym, or classes, or personal trainers to improve their physical fitness? What if you paid similar attention and commitment to supporting and guiding the way you think, feel and behave in a more holistic way? What positive impact could there be on you, your relationships with friends, work colleagues, and others? What negativity could be reduced?

Just imagine how you would feel if you led your life in line with what is important to you, making decisions and behaving in line with these.

> *"On my journey, I have found that the path to self-discovery is the most liberating choice of all."*
> *Muhammad Ali[xv]*

So how can you do this? You might not feel as though you "need" something to guide or help you. Well, we suggest that, in today's high pressure world, it wouldn't do any harm! At one level the answer is simple: you understand yourself, identify what's important and live according to your values – every day. You release the power of your VALUES Superhero. By doing this, you become congruent and realize a sense of flow, feeling happier and a greater sense of fulfilment – authentic happiness. The key aspect to flow is control: in the flow-like state, you exercise control over the contents of your consciousness rather than allowing yourself to be passively determined by external forces.[xvi]

"To be nobody but yourself in a world which is doing its best, day and night, to make you everybody but yourself – means to fight the hardest battle which any human being can fight – and never stop fighting."
E E Cummings[xvii]

At a more complex level, the journey to identify and then live your core values every day is a challenging one; staying on track requires discipline and resilience. Why the approach works is even more complex. The starting point is discovering and connecting with your personal core values: what's really important to you. The next step is to align the way you think, feel and behave.

APPROACH

This is where the my31Practices framework and underpinning methodology plays its part.

The approach is a simple way to help identify and articulate personal values, and then bring these to life through a set of practical behaviours. It is a method based on doing a little every day with mindfulness, internalization, imprinting, and positive reinforcement of your desired behaviour.

We also explore my31Practices through the lens of neuro-linguistic programming (NLP).[xviii] This is the study of subjective experience and contains a range of tools and techniques to help us change unhelpful patterns of behaviour, to build on strengths, and live a life more aligned with our core values, or what is fundamentally important to us.

As you read the various parts and chapters of the book you will see how the components and concepts of NLP support and endorse the my31Practices approach.

Why is my31Practices likely to be effective? We believe that the answer lies in how our bodies work in a holistic way. The heart, mind, body and gut (see Chapter 21 *mBIT*) are enormously important areas in their own right, and experts often focus on one of them to explore in sufficient depth. As a result, they can become viewed as separate "parts" of you, but they are strongly connected and if they are all working together in the same direction, they bring a great source of personal strength.

It was with this in mind, and recognizing the importance of technology in our lives, that the www.my31Practices. com web application was developed and launched, and might be why you are reading this book.

my31Practices has been designed for one thing: to enable people to live their core values in support of their purpose in life. We believe that this approach can result in an increased sense of alignment and congruence, better sustained performance, higher levels of confidence and greater fulfilment. At the same time, it can reduce feelings of uncertainty, helplessness and stress. In summary, my31Practices can release the power of your values for authentic happiness.

PAUSE FOR THOUGHT ...

Why are you reading this book?

WANT TO KNOW MORE?

http://www.my31practices.com/the-book/resources/chapter-2

HOW

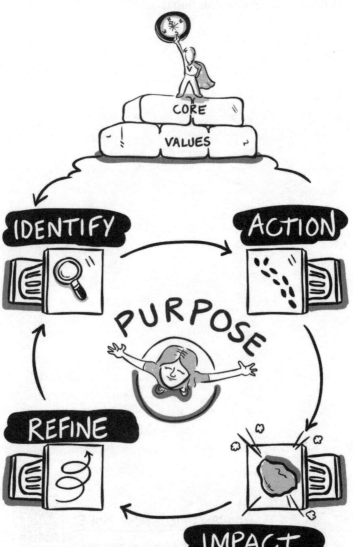

"We know what we are, but not what we may be."
Ophelia in Hamlet[i]

The key to being the best version of yourself starts with your core values; a moral compass guiding you to the way you want to behave. This is more about "how" you do things rather than "what" you do (see Chapter 6 *Values*). In simple terms, when your behaviour is aligned with your values you are happy and, when they are not, you feel stressed (see Chapter 2 *Why*).

However, once you understand your core values, you then need to have the right attitude to bring them to life in your day-to-day behaviour. In this way you can align mind, heart and body in a very powerful combination. This is what my31Practices does. It helps to translate higher-level values into practical behaviours and action. Why 31? Because there are no more than 31 days in a month! The idea is for you to focus on just one myPractice each day so it is easy to do.

"Your mind is the garden, your thoughts are the seeds,
the harvest can either be flowers or weeds."
William Wordsworth[ii]

This is how it works:

FRAMEWORK

The starting point of the framework is purpose; your reason for being. Your core purpose is something that inspires you on an ongoing basis. It should be expressed simply, in a way that engages your heart and mind. Purpose is a topic that warrants a book to itself. While it is not our focus, we want to recognize its importance and connection to the topic of values.

Having identified your purpose, you should support it by your values – in practice – or the way you behave. The 31Practices framework consists of four pillars:

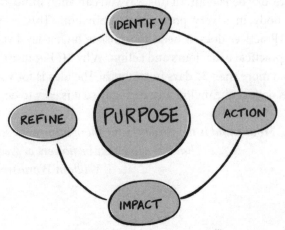

Figure 1. 31Practices Framework[iii]

The framework is based on scientific method and builds from models such as Plan-Do-Check/Study-Act. It is an enquiry-based cycle (identify, action, impact and refine) and will extend understanding and bring individuals closer to their goal.[iv, v] When you use this approach in a practical, meaningful way regularly, it can enable you to make more conscious decisions and to think, feel and act with a greater sense of alignment.

Identify

The first pillar is about identifying your personal core values, which can act as your guide in this ever-changing, complex, and busy world. The values represent what is fundamentally important to you, the "how" you behave in practice. Identifying a set of myPractices that are explicitly connected to these values gives you the opportunity to translate your values into everyday practical, observable behaviours.

Action

The second pillar is putting your core values into action through practice. As a result, habits develop and embed and the values are brought to life in the experiences you have. At the start, this may feel a bit awkward but you'll be surprised at how quickly it becomes much easier until it is just the way you do things.

Impact

The third pillar is to notice what happens as a result of the behaviours that you are practicing. What is the impact on you, on other people, and on your wider environment? How does it make you and other people feel? What are your stories and experiences? Perhaps you learn new things, or reinforce things you were already aware of or had some idea about – or perhaps become more conscious and aware. People who have used the approach tell us that my31Practices brings more connection and alignment with their values. You can read about some of these experiences in Part 4 *Stories*.

Refine

The fourth pillar is to refine and adjust the way in which you are applying your myPractices. In this way, my31Practices is constantly evolving; it's a "living" thing.

On a micro level this could be asking yourself how well did you practice your myPractice today, what did you do well, and what can you do better? On a macro level you could be asking: "Are the myValues and myPractices the best fit, the right sentiment, the best wording?" The values are unlikely to change much from one moment to the next, but as you live with your myValues and myPractices, your increased awareness and insight may develop a different understanding of how to articulate and live them.

The my31Practices framework is designed for you to adapt and apply to suit your own individual style, communities and context. It provides a structure for you to create a set of practical day-to-day behaviours explicitly connected to your personal values, and then supports you to practice these in a sustainable way, every day.

PAUSE FOR THOUGHT ...

How will you start to search for your VALUES Superhero?

WANT TO KNOW MORE?

http://www.my31practices.com/the-book/resources/chapter-3

WHAT

BE THE BEST VERSION OF YOU ☺

REINFORCEMENT   ASSESSMENT

LEARNING   HABIT   PRACTICE

MINDFULNESS   METAPHOR   AFFIRMATION

DAY

EACH

LITTLE

A

DO

FIND YOUR CORE VALUES

"Action is the foundational key to all success."
Pablo Picasso[i]

In Chapters 2 and 3 we explained "why" and "how" the my31Practices approach works, but this will not happen on its own. Nothing will change without you. You need to do something and this means more than reading and thinking; it means taking action. So how do you start and "what" do you need to do?

This is a brief summary of the practical steps you can take. Remember, the choice of how you take this action, and whether you find all of the steps useful, is up to you. The idea is to use my31Practices in the way that works best for YOU. The whole essence of my31Practices is mindful practice or, in other words, making a conscious effort to perform a relevant action as excellently as you can. Mindfulness and each of these other topics below are explored in more detail in Part 2, to give you a more in-depth understanding of the underpinnings of the my31Practices approach.

1. Values

   The first thing to do is set your five core values (my-Values) by identifying what is important to you. A set of five core values which represent the essence of YOU. There are a number of ways to do this, covered in Chapter 6 *Values*.

2. Mindfulness

   This is a fundamental principle of my31Practices; being aware of your behaviour in the present moment and how this can help you make conscious decisions. It's about exercising choices rather than being swept along on a tide of "busyness" and is explored further in Chapter 7 *Mindfulness*.

3. Metaphor

   Once you have identified your values, the next step is to translate these into more practical day-to-day behaviours. People who have used the my31Practices approach tell us that the use of inspirational examples (metaphors), combined with personal life experiences, is a fun and effective way to generate ideas – all will become crystal clear in Chapter 8 *Metaphor*.

4. Affirmation

   When you have chosen your behaviours for each of your myValues, there is a particular style to writing your myPractices. It is a contract with yourself to achieve and reinforce your myPractices through personal ownership, commitment, action orientation, and emotional engagement, covered in Chapter 9 *Affirmation*.

5. Reinforcement

   People who have tried my31Practices tell us they enjoy the feature of being able to choose a quote, a picture and a video that reinforces the message of each myPractice. Reinforcement also comes from the process of reflection – making a conscious effort to reflect on your myPractice each day and recording your actions and the impact they have. These techniques are explored in Chapter 13 *Reinforcement*.

6. Habit

   Because we all lead busy lives, you can easily be distracted by the tide of "busyness". The my31Practices approach is designed to provide support in a number of ways to help you establish a daily routine and structure which eventually becomes natural. This concept is shared in Chapter 11 *Habit*.

7. Practice

   There is a reason the approach is called my31Practices, it's all in the doing. The other elements of my31Practices are designed to help you practice every day. Just do it. The principles of this approach are covered in Chapter 12, *Practice*.

8. Assessment

   There is a common saying, "what gets measured gets done". So measurement and assessment is another valuable feature of the my31Practices approach. There are both quantitative and qualitative measurement features available. Nobody is going to check, so it is completely down to you how you do this and what you score or record. This topic is explored in Chapter 14 *Assessment*.

And that is it, my31Practices: how to BE YOU every day – how to release the power of your values for authentic happiness. It can help you to release the power of your VALUES Superhero. It is designed to be fun, fast and easy to do. At the beginning, it does take some time to identify your myValues and then to create your 31 myPractices, but you do not have to do this in one go. You can start with just one myPractice for each of your five myValues and you're off. Then you can build on this and develop the others as you go. It is a good approach to work towards having a set of 31 myPractices within a two-week period. People who have used my31Practices tell us that during this period they frequently revisit the content and fine tune the wording of their myValues and myPractices until they are happy with them.

> *"Simplicity is the ultimate sophistication."*
> *Leonardo da Vinci[ii]*

Simplicity is at the heart of the my31Practices approach because, at one level, it helps you translate your core values into practical daily behaviours, and then provides you with the support to live these on a day-to-day basis. It is based on doing a little every day with mindfulness, internalization, imprinting and positive reinforcement. It provides you with a discipline for the way you think, feel and behave in much the same way as an exercise programme does for fitness, or a diet plan for weight loss.

Despite the simplicity, the approach is underpinned by a vast array of theories, principles and ideas that have been developed by experts over decades and, in some cases, centuries.

Perhaps most importantly, my31Practices offers flexibility so that your own set of myValues and daily myPractices are designed and driven by you.

PAUSE FOR THOUGHT ...

What is your next step on your my31Practices journey?

WANT TO KNOW MORE?

http://www.my31practices.com/the-book/resources/chapter-4

TEMPLATE

"Seeing is believing.[i]"
English proverb

So far in the book, we have outlined why the my31Practices approach is valuable, how it works, and what you can do to use the approach. In our experience, no matter how good the explanation is, a concrete example is usually very helpful. To make the my31Practices approach "real" here is an example set of myValues, 31 myPractices, and example *myExperiences*:

TRUST
- open, honest and dependable

1. I **deliver** when I agree to do something – or, if this is really not possible, agree the way forward.
    I had agreed to go to the beach with Stan, but it rained so we went to an indoor swimming pool. We had a great time.

2. I do what I **believe** in and **care** about – even when nobody would know or when this is the more difficult option.
    I found an injured bird in the garden and took it to the local vet who said it would recover. My colleague understood why I was delayed.

3. I strive to be **fair** because it is precious.
   I negotiated how my young nieces and nephews shared out the cakes. They were all happy with the outcome.

4. I am **genuine** in my approach and have no time for ulterior motives or short cuts.
   A friend suggested that we could take advantage of another friend leaving the room when playing a board game. I persuaded him that this would not be the right thing to do and if we won the game it would be a hollow victory.

5. I tell the **truth** and trust the same of others.
   I left my mobile number under the windscreen of the car I bumped in the car park. The other driver was incredulous.

6. I value my personal **reputation** as it is my "brand".
   I agreed to speak at an industry event without charging a fee. The organizer was very pleased and I received many kind compliments from the audience.

EXCELLENCE
- delivery of high-quality and ambitious targets

7. I make small **improvements** to be the **best**.
   I improved the wording of myPractice to be more action oriented.

8. I **measure** performance to demonstrate progress.
   I timed my weekend run, which was faster than last month.

9. I put in place the foundation for **sustainable** performance rather than short-lived results.
I offered to establish an ongoing support programme for a client, instead of just delivering the implementation project. They were very impressed and want a proposal.

10. I enjoy **celebrating** achievement with others – with recognition and reward.
I wrote a card congratulating my colleague on her promotion. The smile on her face when she read it is a great memory.

11. I **learn** from the success of others – in spite of being envious sometimes.
I asked a successful author to review our book and they said they would be honoured.

12. I recognize that **alternative views** and input help to deliver the best result.
I made some changes to my website having listened to a student's feedback, and received an immediate compliment.

13. I view failure as valuable when I **learn** from it.
I asked more people than needed for input because of the "drop outs" last time.

14. I work hard and show **persistence** to win – even if this takes a while sometimes.
I followed up with a potential project again for the umpteenth time and they agreed to a meeting.

CREATION
- fresh thinking and relationships
  to bring value

15. I **collaborate** with others to devise and develop innovative ideas and solutions.
    I created an online survey concept in a few hours with a survey expert.

16. I focus on the **value** or benefit of any new idea.
    I kept returning to this point during a meeting about next year's plans for a friend's charity organization. They thanked me for keeping them focused.

17. I turn creative thinking into **practical reality**.
    I proofread the draft manuscript of our book.

18. I seek **fresh thinking** and welcome a similar approach from others.
    I met marketing experts today and asked them what they thought the next trends in customer service would be. Some great ideas to follow up on.

19. I **share** ideas, information and contacts to help other people.
    I introduced two people who both work in the promotions sector. They were both glad to explore further.

20. I agree and communicate sense of **purpose** so everybody understands the "why".
    I did this today in a meeting and it is something that is very natural now.

ADAPTABILITY
- agile adjustment to
  changing circumstances

21. I **embrace change**, focusing energy on what needs to be done next.
    The event next week was cancelled so I have rescheduled the time and booked for the rearranged date.

22. I strive to **think like others for others**: thoughtful gestures to please and impress.
    I brought some macaroons home for the family to enjoy while watching the Roland Garros tennis.

23. I create opportunities to meet and engage with **new people**.
    I agreed to meet a new LinkedIn connection.

24. I recognize and respect **differences** in people but give traditional **courtesy** to all.
    I was introduced to a guy from Finland and reminded myself not to expect too much conversation.

25. I seek out **win-wins** for the best outcome.
    I found a restaurant that suited all of the four people meeting for dinner next week.

26. I grasp opportunities to enjoy **new** experiences, skills and knowledge.
    I learned how to do endnotes.

ENJOYMENT
- visible pleasure and fun

27. I choose **experiences** above material possessions.
I booked a holiday instead of saving for a new car.

28. I share **humour** freely, because I love to hear people **laughing** and see them **smiling**.
I emailed a joke to some people I thought would enjoy it.

29. I **do things** that are enjoyable personally, and for other people.
I sat in the sunshine with a friend for half an hour before catching the train.

30. I **explore** broader **relationships** with people, beyond the task at hand.
I invited a client to a football match to watch their favourite team.

31. I have a **positive** attitude and display genuine **enthusiasm**.
I received some lovely feedback from somebody who said I always bring positive energy.

Through the rest of the book we will explain some of the tools and techniques you can use to create your own set of my31Practices. Remember, there is no "correct" version because everybody has their own unique set. Your my31Practices are individual to you. You may share many, some or none of the above myValues and myPractices.

PAUSE FOR THOUGHT ...

What action will you take today for your behaviour to be aligned with something that is important to you?

WANT TO KNOW MORE?

http://www.my31practices.com/the-book/resources/chapter-5

PART 2

UNDERPINNINGS

This is the part of the book where the various features and thinking of the my31Practices approach are explored, supported by resources for further discovery. Chapters 6–14 deal with how these particular topics support and reinforce the my31Practices approach.

Some chapters are longer, some shorter, there is not a standard approach to the length; just what we felt was "right" for each topic. All of the chapters have a QR code and url leading to additional resources to explore, reference notes to read, or activities to try, and leave you with a thought-provoking question. This is all intended to stimulate exploration, discovery, feeling and thinking. We want the book to be more than just words, and to help inspire you beyond its covers.

VALUES

"It Ain't What You Do (It's the Way That You Do It)"
Fun Boy Three and Bananarama, 1982[i]

The topic of values is gaining increasing attention on a number of levels: organizational, personal, community, societal, political. The "V word" is being used frequently – but what does it mean?

Core values are traits or qualities that represent deeply held beliefs. They reflect what is important to us and what motivates us, and act as guiding principles – a behavioural and decision-making compass.[ii]

Richard Barrett and colleagues differentiate between positive values and potentially limiting values.[iii] Honesty, trust and accountability are positive values, whereas blame, revenge and manipulation are potentially limiting. Positive values are described as virtues and we can draw on them for strength. Potentially limiting values are fear based, evoked when concern for ourselves gets in the way. In this chapter, we focus on positive values.

"Values are the ideals that give meaning to our lives
that are reflected through the priorities we choose
and that we act on consistently and repeatedly."
Brian Hall[iv]

In day-to-day life, values often exist implicitly, under the radar of awareness. The way people behave is a representation of their values and creates their "being". Awareness of your values is a starting point to self-insight and understanding.

You are shaped by what you care about. Where you have a choice, you will choose to do things that enable you to survive and thrive in any situation (see Chapter 17 *Presuppositions*).^v You can use core values to good effect to provide:

- a reference for decision making.
- clarity and increased awareness about individual behaviours (self and others).
- a basis for reflection and enquiry.
- stories for reinforcement.

The result of taking this approach is that you will behave more consistently – viewed from within or from the outside – in an environment which is clearer and less ambiguous. It will help you with "how" you feel, think and behave, as much, if not more than, with "what" you do.

Being aware is a good first step, but no more than that. It is not enough on its own. How do you make sure that you are consistently behaving in line with your values? This is the key question and is also a challenge, especially in such a busy, dynamic world with constant demands on your time and what you do. my31Practices offers a methodology to enable this.

"If I take care of my character,
my reputation will take care of itself."
D L Moody[vi]

The internet and social media have brought a fundamental change with a level of transparency beyond anything you could have imagined 10 or 15 years ago. As a direct result, authenticity is, and will continue to be, increasingly important. Before, it was perhaps possible for people to put on a "front" to tell the story they wanted others to believe, but now it is becoming increasingly difficult to tell a story that is far from the reality. If you don't behave as if your core values matter, then others will not believe they are, in fact, your values – and this can spread far and wide in an instant. More importantly, you run the risk of not living in alignment with your authentic self and the associated consequences (see Chapter 19 *Alignment*). Arguably, this risk is greater in the workplace because of a perceived pressure to give the "right" impression to colleagues. Imagine the positive impact if organizations had a values-based approach to recruitment and selection, performance review, and general employee engagement.

VALUES
and my31Practices

The purpose of my31Practices is to enable you to reconnect with what is important to you, and practice these core values on a daily basis. The my31Practices approach champions authenticity and supports this. It improves your sense of wellbeing with a positive impact on congruence, performance and self-fulfilment, ultimately resulting in authentic happiness.

With my31Practices, the starting point is to identify your top five core values (myValues). Think of these five values as a "set", rather than five separate things, which represents what is really important to you – your essence. There are different ways to do this: you can complete online questionnaires, or start with a long list of values and reduce this down, or you could have a session with a life coach. There are some specific suggestions in the "Want to know more?" section at the end of this chapter to help start your thinking process.

When you have identified your five myValues, the next step is to define what each of them means. The same word could mean different things to different people (see Chapter 20 *Beliefs*). You can see an example of what these myValues and definitions can look like in Chapter 5 *Template*.

Just knowing, or even being able to state your core values, is not sufficient on its own unless you understand how these values can guide your decisions and how they can influence your daily behaviour. my31Practices provides a framework to help you practice behaviours directly linked to your core values every day.

"I am not bound to succeed, but I am bound to live up to what light I have."
Abraham Lincoln[vii]

EXPLORING YOUR PERSONAL VALUES
- in practice

Personal values show up over time in the way people behave. Sometimes it may be difficult to "see" your values when they are so much a part of your everyday world and life. They are sometimes easier to recognize at specific, more extreme moments.

- Think about your peak moments (happiest and/or most successful) – what was going on – what values were "in play" at that time?
- Explore low moments – frustration, misery, failure – what values were being "trampled on" at that time?

What circumstances led to the peak moments or the low moments? What does this say to you about your values?

PAUSE FOR THOUGHT ...

What are your five personal core values (myValues)?

WANT TO KNOW MORE?

http://www.my31practices.com/the-book/resources/chapter-6

MINDFULNESS

"What day is it?" asked Winnie the Pooh.
"It's today," squeaked Piglet.
"My favourite day," said Pooh.
A A Milne[i]

As we are writing this chapter, Johanna Konta became the first British woman to reach a tennis Grand Slam semi-final since 1983 and then went on to win her first Women's Tennis Association title. It is interesting that she puts her success down to the ability to "live in the present". She said: "Rankings come and go, so do results. So that's what has changed. I have taken the expectation away from myself of actually getting results and put it heavily on how I want to be living my life."[ii]

You might have noticed how mindfulness has become "mainstream" and book shops stock many titles on the subject in their personal development sections. Mindfulness practices[iii] are available to everybody and this does not have to involve years of retreats, formal mindfulness programmes,[iv] or several hours of your time every day.[v]

Harvard psychology professor, Ellen Langer, identified a host of qualities that mindful people enjoy more than those who go about their tasks mind*lessly*.[vi] Developments in neuroscience help explain the physical basis for the impact and value of mindfulness practices[vii] and there is increasing evidence that the "cognitive brain" is also the "emotional brain."[viii] Researchers have even found that mindfulness meditation can be an effective method of pain relief.[ix]

Rather than try to create a new one, we are going to explore a definition of mindfulness from a well-respected expert. See what you think of this, and feel free to explore other definitions you find:

"Mindfulness means paying attention in a particular way; on purpose, in the present moment, and non-judgmentally."
Jon Kabat-Zinn

So let's explore the three elements of this definition:

ON PURPOSE

"One man that has a mind and knows it can always beat ten men who haven't and don't."
George Bernard Shaw[x]

Mindfulness involves a conscious direction of our awareness, a clear intention. For example, think of something as simple as walking. As you are striding along, you can consciously focus on the sensations of walking that you are experiencing and your responses to those sensations. From time to time, it is likely that your mind will begin to wander and, if you can notice this, then you can purposefully bring your attention back and refocus on the act of walking.

When you're walking mind*less*ly, you might be aware of what you're doing, but you're probably thinking about lots of other things, and you might be listening to music, using your phone, talking – or all three. So only a very small part of your awareness is focused on walking. You might notice the physical sensations to some extent, but will be even less aware of your thoughts and emotions. Because you're only dimly aware of your thoughts, they might wander. There's no conscious attempt to bring your attention back to your walking. There's no purposefulness.

This purposefulness is a very important part of mindfulness. Having the purpose of staying with your experience, whether it's the breath, or a particular emotion, or something as simple as walking, means that you are actively shaping the mind.

IN THE PRESENT MOMENT

Often your mind wanders through all kinds of thoughts, fast forwarding to an imaginary event in the future, or replaying something from the past. These images spark emotions, which might be positive but can also be negative, expressing sadness, regret, anger, self-pity, etc. As you entertain these kinds of thoughts, you reinforce the emotions and can make yourself miserable. But how valuable are these thoughts? Well, the past is gone and no longer exists, and the future is just in your imagination until it arrives. The one moment you can experience is the present – and when you are living in the past or the future, you are less aware of what is happening to you in this moment.

Peter Senge and his colleagues describe "presence"[xi] as full consciousness, being fully aware in the present moment and open to what might emerge, beyond assumptions normally held. Presence is also about letting go of old identities and the need for control. These aspects together allow things to emerge – "letting come".

Some see presence and the capacity for reflection as the true attribute of wisdom.[xii] Mindful presence can enable us to see that information is contextual rather than truthful or "fact".

> *"Yesterday's the past, tomorrow's the future,*
> *but today is a gift. That's why it's called the present."*
> *Bil Keane[xiii]*

NON-JUDGMENTALLY

> *"Whatever the present moment contains,*
> *accept it as if you had chosen it."*
> *Eckhart Tolle[xiv]*

Kabat-Zinn's definition highlights that an important aspect of mindfulness is acceptance. This means being able to be aware of your experience without either clinging to it or pushing it away. Instead you accept your experience with equanimity, like an impartial observer. This doesn't necessarily mean that you want to stay the way you are at the moment. On the contrary, you almost certainly will want to move on, but the first step in moving on is to recognize fully where you are, and to accept it.

Resist the temptation to judge the experience as good or bad. Or if you do make those judgments, simply notice them and let go of them. Whether it's pleasant or painful, treat the event the same way. Don't be upset because you're experiencing something you don't want to be experiencing, or because you're not experiencing what you would rather be experiencing. Simply accept whatever arises. Observe it mindfully. Notice it arriving, passing, and disappearing.

> *"Feelings come and go like clouds in a windy sky.*
> *Conscious breathing is my anchor."*
> Thích Nhất Hạnh[xv]

Greater mindfulness enables us to bring ourselves back to now, and make more skilful choices about how we want to respond in the moment – choosing how we want to feel, what we want to think, and how we behave.

BEFRIENDING YOUR DISTRACTIONS

One way to develop acceptance is to be aware of your emotions in a spirit of friendly curiosity. Imagine saying or thinking, "It's OK to feel like this," or "Why am I feeling like this?" By taking this approach, the vicious cycle of feeling bad about feeling bad is broken.

The same thing applies to your thoughts and emotions, and you can consciously recognize that your thoughts are not reality. When you notice thoughts arising, you can let go of the stream of thought, and by letting go, you are stopping it from continuing or growing bigger.

Another technique you can use to remind yourself that your thoughts are interpretations and not necessarily facts is to remind yourself (perhaps out loud) that a thought is no more than a thought, to question how and why you made that interpretation, and ask the question, "What else could that mean?" This can give you a surprising sense of freedom. Just give it a try to see how it works for you.

> *"Be curious, not judgmental."*
> *Walt Whitman[xvi]*

Having said all of the above, this is not to say that a focus on the present means that you should never think about the past or the future. Of course, your past experiences can be of great value, as can looking forward, to create the best possibilities in the future. What can be stressful, though, is all the mindless, negative evaluations you make and the worry that you'll find problems and not be able to solve them. "What you want is a soft openness – to be attentive to the things you're doing but not single-minded, because then you're missing other opportunities."[xvii]

> *"Do every act of your life as though it were*
> *the very last act of your life."*
> *Marcus Aurelius[xviii]*

MINDFULNESS
and my31Practices

Using my31Practices helps you to have a mindful approach to your core values by paying attention: on purpose, in the present moment, and non-judgementally.

You can set up your day with intention by taking five minutes to read your myPractice for the day, together with your chosen quote, photo and videoclip – or if you don't have them already, choose them. People who have used my31Practices have told us that this purposeful intent means that, suddenly, you see things that you would not have seen and you are ready and prepared to act – so you do. Then, taking responsibility for what you do with your myPractice today brings it to the present moment. Finally, at the end of each day, you can reflect on, in a non-judgemental way, how well you "lived" the myPractice and the impact on you, other people and the wider environment.

Over time, focusing on one myPractice at a time builds strong habits (see Chapter 11 *Habit*) and because these are explicitly connected to your values, you are, by definition, living your values – in practice.

By the way, we have to admit that this idea of one practice at a time is not an original approach to awakening or enlightenment. When writing the first book, *The 31 Practices,* we came across *37 Practices of the Bodhisattva,*[xix] which was written in a cave near Ngulchu Rinchen in the 14th century by a monk, a teacher of scripture and reasoning, for his own and others' benefit!

MINDFULNESS
- in practice

> *"Mindfulness isn't difficult,*
> *we just need to remember to do it."*
> *Sharon Salzberg[xx]*

When you have a feeling, locate the feeling in the body, and then in the spirit of playful curiosity, choose any or all of the following questions:

Where exactly is it located?
What shape is it?
What colour – if any – is it?
What kind of texture does it have?
Does it change over time?
What name could you give it?

By describing the emotion in this way, you realize that it is smaller than you are. You're bigger than any emotion that you experience, which means that if you stand back from the emotion then not everything you're experiencing is coloured by the emotion. In this way you create a sort of "space" between yourself and the emotion so that you're not so caught up in it.

PAUSE FOR THOUGHT ...

What thoughts and feelings are you noticing right now?

WANT TO KNOW MORE?

http://www.my31practices.com/the-book/resources/chapter-7

METAPHOR

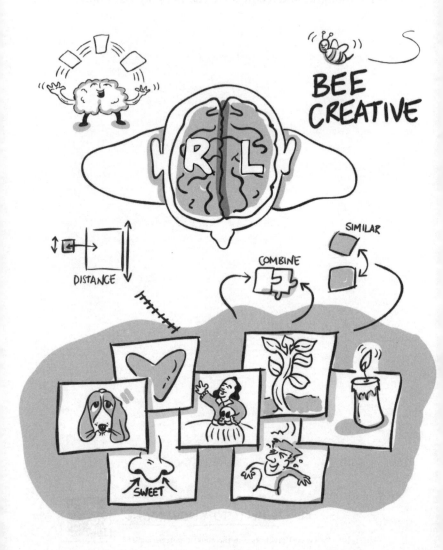

"While a picture might be worth a thousand words, a metaphor is worth a thousand pictures.[i]"
Daniel Pink

It may, or may not be a bolt from the blue for you to know that we tune in to a chorus of opinion from people who think there is a veil of mystery about what a "metaphor" is. And yet the English language is peppered with everyday examples such as "the sweet smell of success", "the bitter end", "peace of mind", "loose cannon", "food for thought", "broken heart" and "leap of faith". There is also fogginess over the difference between metaphors and similes, so we thought it would be a good place to start this chapter by trying to put things straight.

By the way, how many metaphors are there in the above paragraph?

In simple terms, a metaphor shows one thing represented as another. The word originates from the Greek word *metaphorá*, meaning to transfer, to carry over. This technique can expand the way we see things, often heightening our perception to make concepts richer, deeper and/or more accessible.

SIMILE IS LIKE METAPHOR

You may be wondering what difference there is, if any, between similes and metaphors, so we want to have a go at explaining this. Because similes and metaphors both make comparisons, all similes are metaphors – but not all metaphors are similes. Both similes and metaphors use a vivid image to help people understand and also remember a concept or idea; everyone "gets it"– the light bulb goes on.

The key difference is that similes compare one thing with another, highlighting the comparison by using the words "like" or "as". The process of comparison involves your more rational brain, your thinking processes.

Metaphors, on the other hand, go a step further by turning one thing into something else. They bypass your rational brain and shortcut to your imagination, senses and emotions. By doing this, they somehow achieve a higher and deeper level of understanding and appreciation – through a phrase that isn't true!!

> *"A metaphor is a compacted version of reality."*
> *Rick Eigenbrod[ii]*

Let's use one of our favourite stories, Forrest Gump,[iii] to show the practical difference between a simile and a metaphor:

In the film, Forrest Gump said, "My momma always said, 'Life was like a box of chocolates. You never know what you're gonna get.'" Because the word "like" is used, this is a simile.

In the book, Forrest says, "Bein' a' idiot is no box of chocolates." This is a metaphor because it makes the direct comparison between being an idiot and a box of chocolates.

> *"The brain is wider than the sky."*
> *Emily Dickinson[iv]*

POWER, METAPHORICALLY SPEAKING

In this chapter, we are exploring metaphors because it is a technique people have told us works well with my31Practices. Metaphors conjure up vivid images and allow us to "see" things from a new perspective, so they are useful tools for creative thinking. You probably agree with this point of view intuitively just from your personal experience of thinking in images when you dream. But we are in good company – Aristotle considered the use of metaphor to be a sign of genius. He believed that individuals who could identify resemblances between two separate areas of existence and link them together had special gifts and said, "The greatest thing by far is to be a master of metaphor."[v]

Studies in cognitive science have reinforced the importance of metaphor, demonstrating that our ordinary
conceptual system, in terms of which we both think and
act, is fundamentally metaphorical in nature.[vi]

Cognitive linguists George Lakoff and Mark Johnson write,
"A metaphor may thus be a guide for future action. Such
actions will, of course, fit the metaphor. This will, in turn,
reinforce the power of the metaphor to make experience
coherent. In this sense metaphors can be self-fulfilling
prophecies." Metaphors are powerful indeed!

And the passing of time has not diluted their importance.
Best-selling author Daniel Pink says: "In a complex world,
mastery of metaphor has become ever more valuable.
Human thought processes are largely metaphorical.
Metaphor making is critical – metaphorical imagination is
essential in forging empathetic connections and communicating experiences that others do not share. A large part
of self-understanding is the search for appropriate personal metaphors that make sense of our lives. The more we
understand metaphor, the more we understand ourselves".
[vii] These words are particularly relevant for and supportive
of the my31Practices approach. Thank you, Daniel.

> *"The world is emblematic. Parts of speech are*
> *metaphors, because the whole of nature*
> *is a metaphor of the human mind."*
> *Ralph Waldo Emerson[viii]*

HOW DO METAPHORS WORK?

The reason that metaphors are so powerful is that they can make the strange familiar, and the familiar strange. When you experiment with the metaphor, it allows you to transfer your understanding from what you are familiar with to what you are less familiar with. They help you to appreciate something in a new light and see a fresh perspective in three ways:

1. By identifying similarities between two different concepts, ideas or challenges.

2. By examining something in a new context.

3. By creating distance from your current situation (what you know, as well as your comfort zone).

When you use a metaphor to link two ideas together, you are combining elements that have little or no logical connection. By breaking the rules of logic in this way, metaphors can open up the creative side of the brain – the part that is stimulated by images, ideas, and concepts. So metaphorical thinking can help you with creative problem solving: to use another famous metaphor, it helps you "think outside the box". Don't get too hung up on how well the metaphorical example maps back. The whole idea is to generate ideas that you might not have otherwise thought of, so just let the ideas flow without too much judgement.

Inventor and psychologist, William J J Gordon, formalized the metaphor process during the 1950s as Synectics, when he learned through research that people often solved problems creatively when they expressed the issue or need as a metaphor.

METAPHOR
and my31Practices

Using metaphors might help you to identify your myPractices to reflect your personal values. It is a very simple and fun process where you think of the very best example you can of your chosen value. This could be a person, an organization, or a scenario: for example, if your value is "success", you can choose a winning sports team, individual, or successful company. The important thing is that you think it is a fantastic example representing the meaning of your value. You then consider the behaviours that you associate with your example that makes it such a good representation of your chosen value. If your example of success is an Olympic gold medallist, you might list things such as measuring performance, using the best equipment, a disciplined approach to diet, investment in training, studying high performers, breaking down an activity into steps, etc. Think of as many behaviours as you can, always with the metaphor in mind. You then review your "longlist", this time with the mindset of "Which of these behaviours could I adopt or adapt to best represent my personal value? What would make me really proud if I did these things?"

Choose your favourite six behaviours for each of your five myValues and these will make up your 30 myPractices. In case you're wondering what happens about myPractice 31, you can use "I choose my favourite myPractice and practice". If you prefer to create another myPractice instead, that works too. You can see an example set of my31Practices in Chapter 4, *Template*.

METAPHOR
- in practice

Perhaps the most widespread use of metaphor is in literature and song-writing, and we would like to share some of our favourites with you:

"All the world's a stage, and all the men and women merely players." William Shakespeare[ix]

"All our words are but crumbs that fall down from the feast of the mind." Khalil Gibran[x]

"Let us be grateful to people who make us happy, they are the charming gardeners who make our souls blossom." Marcel Proust[xi]

"Fill your paper with the breathings of your heart." William Wordsworth[xii]

And what about these metaphors from songs you may recognize:

"Your candle burned out long before
Your legend ever did"[xiii]
From.. by ....

"You ain't nothin' but a hound dog
Quit snoopin' 'round my door"[xiv]
From.. by ....

"Cause, baby, you're a firework
Come on, show'em what you're worth"[xv]
From.. by ....

What are your own favourites?

PAUSE FOR THOUGHT ...

If you were a musical artist or group of musicians, what group would you want to be? What would be the style of your music and lyrics? How would you behave and what would your fans say about you?

What kind of values would you be portraying as this artist or band? How do these translate into your personal values?

AND?

By the way, for us, this book is a handle on the door between what you know and what you may be becoming more curious about – and there are 14 metaphors in the first paragraph of this chapter. The answers to the song lyric metaphors are in the end notes for this chapter (at the very back of the book).

WANT TO KNOW MORE?

http://www.my31practices.com/the-book/resources/chapter-8

AFFIRMATION

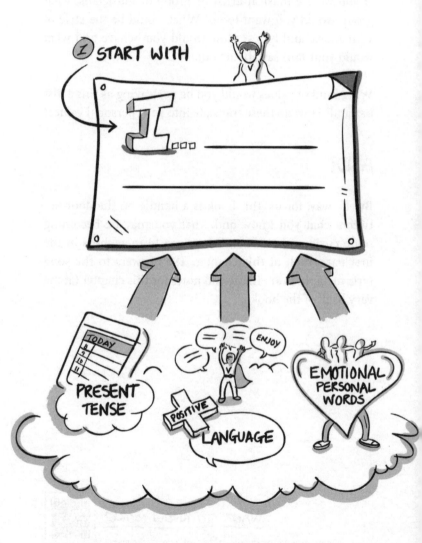

"I figured that if I said it enough, I would convince the world that I really was the greatest."
Muhammad Ali[i]

An affirmation is defined as a statement or proposition that is declared to be true.[ii] Self-affirmations were first popularized by French psychologist Émile Coué[iii] back in the 1920s, so they have been around for some time.

Proponents of the "law of attraction"[iv] often credit self-affirmations as being capable of magnetically drawing positive things such as financial success, love, and renewed health to us. In this chapter, it is not our intention to discuss the law of attraction. Our belief is that the act of creating a set of myPractices in this affirmation style plays an important part in helping them to be effective. But we also believe that it is even more important to take action as well.

Here is an explanation of why the affirmation approach is effective by Manprit Kaur – we love the clear focus on practice:

"Remember, by making affirmations, you are consciously programming your mind to think in a certain way, so that hopeful and happy thinking becomes a part of your being. Affirmations are a way to train the mind; and training happens when you practice, practice, practice! Training requires conscious effort, discipline, belief, and consistency. That is exactly how you need to practice your affirmations."[v]

> *"As a man thinketh in his heart, so is he."*
> Proverbs 23:7

WHAT DO THEY LOOK LIKE?

Affirmations are statements that are designed to create self-change in the person using them or to reinforce current wanted behaviour. They can operate at a number of levels (a simple reminder, inspiration, focusing attention) with the potential to develop and embed positive and sustained change. Over time it becomes natural.

Four Guidelines for Effective Affirmations

1. First person: begin your affirmations with "I". This makes your statements personal, and easy for you to associate with and take responsibility for.

   "I think I can. I think I can. I think I can. I know I can."
   The Little Engine That Could by Watty Piper [vi]

2. Present tense: write your affirmations as if they are already happening. This means saying, "I offer thoughtful gestures to people" rather than "I will offer thoughtful gestures to people". The present tense is far more compelling than the future tense, where you can find reasons that this is not what happens right now. For a similar reason, avoid using the phrase "try to" – this creates an

opportunity for you to find an excuse or reason not to do something and weakens your commitment.

> *"Do. Or do not. There is no try."*
> *Yoda, The Empire Strikes Back[vii]*

3. Positive language: focus on what you want to do rather than what you do not want to do. For example "I enjoy making healthy choices when eating" rather than "I no longer eat fast foods".

4. Emotional, personal words: these positive emotions are powerful motivators. For a similar reason, use specific words or phrases that you use or relate to. For example "I hang out with my pals to feel happy" rather than "I spend time with my friends," which sounds impersonal and like a bit of a chore.

> *"Words can inspire and words can destroy. Choose yours well."*
> *Robin Sharma[viii]*

HOW DO YOU USE THEM?

We believe that the daily discipline of my31Practices is an important factor. But, what is more important than what we believe or think, as with all of the my31Practices features, is what works best for you. Different people have different preferences.

"Affirmation without discipline is the beginning of delusion."
Jim Rohn[ix]

This is why you can set your myPractices reminder at a time to suit you. Then we suggest that you take some quiet time to focus on your myPractice for the day. You might like to write it down, highlight the key words, repeat it out loud, leave notes, or associated quotes around the house. Then at the end of the day before you sleep, spend some time considering your myPractice and your experiences during the day. Just take five minutes to try these things for one or two days and see what differences you notice.

DO THEY WORK?

There is a range of opinion in recent research. On the one hand, some researchers suggest the benefits of using affirmations include:

- protection against the damaging effects of stress on problem-solving performance.
- fostering better problem solving.
- helping deal with threats to our self-integrity.

People can be affirmed by engaging in activities that remind them of "who they are": doing so reduces their need for defensive responses when faced with implications for self-integrity in threatening events. There is a connection here with Chapter 21 *mBIT*.

There are other researchers who cite the lack of supporting scientific evidence and see possible advantages and disadvantages for different groups of people.

Another school of thought focusses on mindfulness and a commitment to an alignment of values and behaviour (see Chapter 7 *Mindfulness*).

AND?

So where do all of these seemingly contradictory points of view take us? Well, we believe it can all be distilled down to the following:

Affirmations by themselves might be of some value to some people, but, when used as part of a broader approach (alongside other techniques such as mindfulness, practice, recognition and reward, reinforcement and others) can be a powerful approach to the way you think, behave and feel. Perhaps we should invent a new word: Affirmactions.

> *"First say to yourself what you would be;*
> *and then do what you have to do."*
> *Epictetus[x]*

AFFIRMATION
- in practice

Here's a chance to design and craft your own affirmation, using the four guidelines for effective affirmations above:

I ....
....

This could become one of your myPractices.

PAUSE FOR THOUGHT ...

What are your views on whether affirmations are powerful in themselves, or if they need to be supported by actions as well?

WANT TO KNOW MORE?

http://www.my31practices.com/the-book/resources/chapter-9

LEARNING

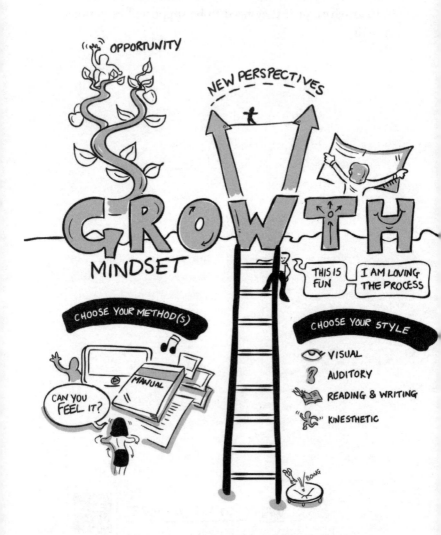

"Nothing you can do, but you can learn how to be you in time.
It's easy.[i]"
The Beatles

Because of its common use in everyday language, "learning" is one of those words that can easily be underestimated in terms of its complexity – as we found out when we were researching the topic.

Psychologists often define learning as a relatively permanent change in behaviour as a result of experience. The psychology of learning focuses on a range of topics related to how people learn and interact with their environments.[ii] We like the added dimension of motivation: "including both observable activity and internal processes such as thinking, attitudes and emotions".[iii]

How do different people learn? Well, there is no agreed answer. In educational psychology, there are many differing perspectives, e.g. behavioural, cognitive, developmental, social cognitive and constructivist.[iv] You might be surprised to learn that there are at least 71 different learning style schemes, each containing multiple learning style types.[v] They classify learners into styles using a variety of different methods – but the validity of all of these theories has been questioned and criticized.[vi]

It is not our intention to explore all of the various learning styles or any of them in great depth. In this chapter, we will highlight some expert thinking on the topic of learning, together with our own ideas where we think it relates to the my31Practices approach. We also explore one topic separately in Chapter 13 *Reinforcement*.

At a simple level, we support the concept of holistic learning theory: the basic premise is that the: "individual personality consists of many elements ... specifically ... the intellect, emotions, the body impulse (or desire), intuition and imagination that all require activation if learning is to be more effective".[vii] There is a connection here with the importance of perception, explored in Chapter 16 *Maps*. We also believe in the value of recognizing differences in the way each individual may learn best, and considering these principles of learning to design the most effective and enjoyable approach.

LEARNING
and my31Practices

The my31Practices approach draws upon a whole range of learning theories and styles.

Sensory Stimulation Theory

Traditional sensory stimulation theory has the basic premise that effective learning occurs when the senses are stimulated.[viii] Distinguished author and consultant, Dugan Laird, quotes research that found that the vast majority of knowledge held by adults (75%) is learned through seeing. By stimulating the senses, especially the visual sense, learning can be enhanced. This theory also says that if multi-senses are stimulated, greater learning takes place (see Chapter 16 *Maps*).

However, the emphasis on visual sense seems to be contradicted by other research which shows that sense of smell is especially effective as reminders of past experience.[ix]

> *"Tell me and I forget. Teach me and I remember.*
> *Involve me and I learn."*
> *Benjamin Franklin*[x]

Teacher Neil Fleming's VARK model[xi] identifies different learning preferences based on our senses: visual learning (pictures, video, diagrams), auditory learning (music, discussion, lectures), reading and writing (making lists, reading, taking notes), or kinesthetic learning (touching and doing, experiments, hands-on activities).

Do you recognize your learning preferences? What are they? Of course, you might prefer to learn using more than one of these styles and if you change preferences based on the situation, or the type of information you are learning, then you have what is referred to as a multimodal style. When you visit the my31Practices website you will see that you can read your myPractice, add a quotation, a video clip and a picture. This integrated, multiple approach is described somewhat grandly as "a synergistic advantage through juxtaposition"[xii]... but we have not worked out how you can add a smell yet, so all suggestions are welcome!

Experiential learning

Educational theorist David Kolb's research found that people learn in four ways, with the likelihood of developing one mode of learning more than another.[xiii] The process can begin at any of the stages and is continuous, i.e. there is no limit to the number of cycles you can make in a learning situation. The theory asserts that without reflection we would simply continue to repeat our mistakes.

> *"He who learns but does not think, is lost!*
> *He who thinks but does not learn is in great danger."*
> *Confucius[xiv]*

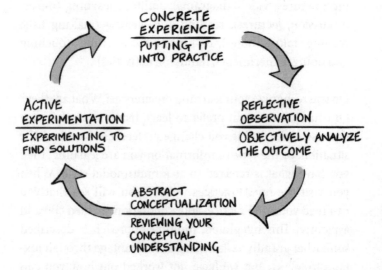

CONCRETE
EXPERIENCE
PUTTING IT
INTO PRACTICE

REFLECTIVE
OBSERVATION
OBJECTIVELY ANALYZE
THE OUTCOME

ABSTRACT
CONCEPTUALIZATION
REVIEWING YOUR
CONCEPTUAL
UNDERSTANDING

ACTIVE
EXPERIMENTATION
EXPERIMENTING TO
FIND SOLUTIONS

Figure 2. The experiential learning cycle

With my31Practices, the process starts with identifying your personal values and then translating these into a set of myPractices to review your conceptual understanding. The active experimentation stage happens each day as you look for opportunities and ways to use the myPractice for the day. Then, when you put your myPractice into practice you have a concrete experience. Finally, the reminder at the end of the day encourages reflective observation with rating your performance and by capturing your myExperiences.

> *"Life is a series of experiences, each one of which makes us bigger, even though sometimes it is hard to realize this. For the world was built to develop character, and we must learn that the setbacks and grieves which we endure help us in our marching onward."*
> *Henry Ford[xv]*

Cognitive-Gestalt approaches

The myExperience focus of my31Practices is also closely related to this approach where the emphasis is on the importance of experience, meaning, problem solving and the development of insights.[xvi] The creators of neuro-linguistic programming, John Grinder and Richard Bandler, were greatly influenced by the work of Fritz Perls, founder of Gestalt Therapy (see Chapter 15 *NLP*). We believe that it is the process of rating and recording the experience that is important, rather than the score itself or the details of the myExperience. This is because you might have different needs and concerns at different times, and also because you will have subjective interpretations in different contexts.

> *"Learning never exhausts the mind."*
> *Leonardo da Vinci[xvii]*

Action Learning

Whereas the cognitive-Gestalt approaches focus on developing insights, the Action Learning approach links the world of learning with the world of action.

The "father" of Action Learning, Reg Revans, has said that there can be no learning without action and no (sober and deliberate) action without learning and uses this equation: L(learning) = P(programmed knowledge) + Q (questioning insight)

> *"You don't learn to walk by following rules. You learn by doing, and by falling over."*
> *Richard Branson [xviii]*

In education environments, Action Learning is achieved through a reflective process within small co-operative learning groups known as "action learning sets."[xix] The sets meet regularly to work on individual members' real-life issues with the aim of learning with, and from, each other. Revans, and others, argued that Action Learning is ideal for finding solutions to problems that do not have a "right" answer because the necessary questioning insight can be facilitated by people learning with and from each other in action learning sets. We believe the essence of this approach is highly relevant for my31Practices: a focus on practice, conscious insight and learning followed by further practice. The key difference is that when you use the my31Practices approach you apply it individually, rather than in groups, but perhaps a development of my31Practices will be to connect people with the same values so they can form "action learning sets".

This learner and experience centred approach is very much in keeping with the thinking behind adult learning: "By adulthood people are self-directing. This is the concept that lies at the heart of andragogy – andragogy is therefore student-centred, experience-based, problem-oriented and collaborative, very much in the spirit of the humanist approach to learning and education. The whole educational activity turns on the student".[xx]

SO WHAT?

Having an understanding of these different ways in which people learn is helpful and there is another closely related topic which we believe has a huge impact on successful learning outcomes. At the beginning of this chapter we mentioned the importance of motivation and the related topic of mindset.

This is a simple idea discovered by professor of psychology Carol Dweck in decades of research on achievement and success.[xxi]

In a fixed mindset, people believe their basic qualities, such as their intelligence or talent, are simply fixed traits. They spend their time documenting their intelligence or talent instead of developing them. They also believe that talent alone creates success – without effort. Dweck shares why she believes these people are wrong as follows.

In a growth mindset, people believe that their most basic abilities can be developed through dedication and hard work – brains and talent are just the starting point. This view creates a love of learning and a resilience that is essential for great achievement. Dweck suggests that virtually all great people have had these qualities.

Teaching a growth mindset creates motivation and productivity in the worlds of business, education, and sports. It enhances relationships.

This growth mindset concept is highly relevant to my31Practices. At the beginning, there is the anchoring of the values and creating the set of my31Practices but, beyond this, not much is predictable. my31Practices encourages a growth mindset because so little is "known" and there is so much that can emerge. The way in which the myPractice is applied each day is down to you being prepared with your myPractice at the front of your mind, recognizing an opportunity when it arises and then conscious practice. If you consider a simple example with the myPractice "I offer help to a stranger" and a lady opening her purse and spilling coins on the floor. The end result is that she is grateful for your help to rescue her coins, you have an engaging conversation, and you feel good about yourself. Others may also have witnessed what happened and be more likely to respond in a similar manner in future. Finally, what could be the positive impact of this story being told by everyone involved? A positive outcome all round – but this could not have been predicted and, arguably, if it hadn't been for your myPractice, the "event" would not have happened at all.

In this example, you have followed a sequence of action in line with what is important to you, good intention, practice and learning as you go. In other words, the 31Practices Framework (see Chapter 3 *How*).

> *"The beautiful thing about learning is that no one can take it away from you."*
> *B B King*[xxii]

LEARNING
- in practice

Embrace a growth mindset by attempting something you don't know how to do, exploring something unknown, or reading a magazine you have never read before, with a positive attitude. What happens as a result of your "adventure"?

PAUSE FOR THOUGHT ...

What style of learning do you find most effective and/or enjoyable and does this change according to particular situations?

WANT TO KNOW MORE?

http://www.my31practices.com/the-book/resources/chapter-10

HABIT

"Excellence is an art won by training and habituation: we do not act rightly because we have virtue or excellence, but we rather have these because we have acted rightly; 'these virtues are formed in man by his doing the actions'; we are what we repeatedly do. Excellence, then, is not an act, but a habit."
Will Durant[i]

This introduction quote is often mistakenly attributed to philosopher and scientist Aristotle and used in a shorter form. We think that this full version is a much better explanation of how your actions become what you are. Clearly, what you repeatedly do is therefore of critical importance and we owe our thanks to Wikipedia for what we think is a great definition to open this chapter:

A habit (or wont) is a routine of behaviour that is repeated regularly and tends to occur subconsciously.[ii, iii, iv]

In the *American Journal of Psychology* (1903) it is defined in this way: "A habit, from the standpoint of psychology, is a more or less fixed way of thinking, willing, or feeling acquired through previous repetition of a mental experience." [iii] Habitual behaviour often goes unnoticed in persons exhibiting it, because a person does not need to engage in self-analysis when undertaking routine tasks. Habits are sometimes compulsory.[iv] The process by which new behaviours become automatic is habit formation. Old habits are hard to break and new habits are hard to form, because the behavioural patterns we repeat are imprinted in our neural pathways,[v] but it is possible to form new habits through repetition.[vi]

> *"If you create an act, you create a habit. If you create a habit, you create a character. If you create a character, you create a destiny."*
> André Maurois[vii]

So how do you establish a habit and embed the behaviour? Two models in this space have many similarities but also some differences:

Figure 3. The Hook Model[viii]

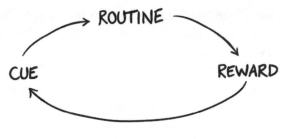

Figure 4. The Habit Loop[ix]

You will see that both models involve a trigger or cue, followed by an action or routine and have a reward element. The Hook Model includes the additional concept of user investment. There are two parts to this: first the IKEA effect,[x] that you perceive more value in something where you have made a contribution and are emotionally engaged (e.g. Facebook posts); the other aspect is that since people are creatures of habit, your investment in a habit creates a form of inertia that makes it increasingly unlikely that you will look for a new solution to your need.

NUDGE

What both models agree on is the importance of the prompt or cue, so let's explore this further.

It is a perhaps surprisingly widespread reference that the average person has "70,000 thoughts per day."[xi] Behavioural psychologist Daniel Kahneman[xii] and researchers refer to psychological presents of 3 seconds (600,000 in a month) and physician and wellness expert Deepak Chopra[xiii] mentions "60,000 to 80,000" thoughts each day, so there is some uncertainty about the accuracy of the number. There are also questions about what a thought is in the first place and the relevance of waking/sleeping hours. What seems clear to us is that, whatever the number, your brain is a busy organ. This makes for an incessant and almost limitless range of options and possibilities from which you are making choices and decisions all the time, every day – a snowstorm of options providing the perfect conditions for some poor decision making.

So how can you equip yourself to perform (and be) at your best? The answer may lie in prompts and practice.

Drawing on decades of cutting-edge behavioural science research, Richard H Thaler and Cass R Sunstein's renowned book, *Nudge,*[xiv] offers an insightful perspective on how to improve the decisions you make in everything you do. *Nudge* is about choices. It demonstrates how you will be able to successfully nudge yourself to make the best decisions for you by learning about choice architecture.

Psychologists have also found that what distinguishes people with great expertise is not that they have more answers than others, but they are more adept at situational recognition and more intentional about their decision-making processes.[xv] The recognition-primed decision (RPD) process highlights how decisions made under pressure, time constraints, and shifting conditions involve three main steps:

1. Experiencing the situation
2. Analyzing the situation
3. Implementing the decision

The process highlights how important pattern recognition and past experience are for making instant decisions. Chapter 12 *Practice* explores how you can achieve this.

PROMPTS

"I wanted only to live in accord with the promptings which came from my true self. Why was that so very difficult?"
Hermann Hesse[xvii]

Depending on your age, you might have heard stories from your grandparents about them tying a knot in a handkerchief to remind them of something. Paper tissues have all but ended this practice, but reminders are still very powerful and common spread. You won't be shocked to learn that there is scientific evidence that reminders and behavioural nudges do in fact work.[xvii] While often simple and straightforward, their power should not be underestimated. Just think of examples in your own life:

- Facebook encourages you to log in habitually.
- Rosetta Stone nudges (or pushes) you to learn languages effectively.
- Video games challenge you to make the next level.
- The ping of your phone announces the arrival of a message and prompts you to look at it straight away.

By you for you

Many of these examples above are created by external forces, but you can use the same technique to nudge yourself – like you use online calendars to nudge you to remember appointments and be on time. Here are some examples and there is space in the introduction illustration to add some more of your own.

Note to self

Leaving yourself a handwritten note or checklist is a great reminder for both short-term tasks and long-term goals.[xviii] You can leave these prompts where you will see them, perhaps regularly, during the day. Text messages or emails can be used in a similar way.

Share your story

Communicating with other people will help in two ways: it will help you to remember what had been on your mind and it will increase the chances of you doing something in practice. The more you discuss the ideas and thoughts that are significant to you, the better you will focus your attention and channel your energies to doing them.

Mindfulness triggers

You can also consciously remind yourself to be mindful whenever a specific event occurs. For example, when the phone rings, you can remind yourself to take your awareness to your breathing, to sit up straight (or even stand), to smile, and to breathe deeply three times before you answer.

You can even associate a phrase or image with a trigger – for example, you could say to yourself "opening my heart" as you open the door to your house after a day at work, or picture yourself with a large pair of ears as you sit down for a meeting, to remind you to listen.

> *"Moral excellence comes about as a result of habit. We become just by doing just acts, temperate by doing temperate acts, brave by doing brave acts."*
> *Aristotle[xix]*

HABIT
and my31Practices

Once you have set up your myValues and myPractices, you will see for yourself that the principles of these habit models are present in the my31Practices approach:

- At the beginning of each day, you receive a prompt to remind you of your myPractice for the day (Prompt/Cue).
- When you view this on myHub (Action/Routine), you can read the myPractice and see the supporting picture you have used (Prompt/Cue).
- Take the time to (Prompt/Cue) look at the quote and video you have chosen (Action/Routine).
- You may also be pleased with the way your myPractice reads (Reward). If you haven't chosen a picture, quote,

or video yet, why not choose one each day until they are complete (Investment)?

- At the end of each day you receive another reminder (Prompt/Cue) to rate your "performance" and capture your myExperience prompting you to reflect and record this (Action/Routine).
- Completing this "process" is motivating because you are confirming to yourself that you completed your myPractice, to whatever extent (Reward). This happens on two levels: first, the scoring process which might be an obvious reward or sense of achievement; at another level, recording your experience reinforces it (Reward) and the accumulation of this data over time builds your connection with the my31Practices approach (Investment).
- Sharing your ratings and/or myExperience serves a similar purpose (Reward and Investment).

Finally, but importantly, the my31Practices approach is based on the principle of "baby steps"[xx] – just one small thing each day, so it's easy to do as part of your everyday life.

HABIT
- in practice

To demonstrate the power of habit and simple prompts, try removing a reminder from your daily life: if you always keep your car keys in a bowl on a piece of furniture near your front door, put them somewhere else for a while. See what happens, how you feel and what impact this has on you and perhaps other people, who you may accuse of moving your keys.

PAUSE FOR THOUGHT ...

What small "nudge" experiment will you try – and when will you do this?

WANT TO KNOW MORE?

http://www.my31practices.com/the-book/resources/chapter-11

PRACTICE

"Only one thing registers on the subconscious mind: repetitive application – practice. What you practice is what you manifest."
Fay Weldon[i]

Practice is about applying an idea, belief, or method rather than the theories related to it. In the words of Mahatma Gandhi,[ii] *"An ounce of practice is worth more than tons of preaching"*. Practice in this chapter is also about repeatedly performing an activity to become skilled in it.[iii] As you may have guessed, practice is probably the most fundamental single element of the my31Practices approach.

"Practice is a means of inviting the perfection desired."
Martha Graham[iv]

Think of tennis players Martina Navratilova and Novak Djokovic, ice hockey player Wayne Gretsky, Formula One driver Michael Schumacher, gymnast Olga Korbut, American football's Joe Montana, soccer's Cristiano Ronaldo, or athletes Jackie Joyner-Kersee and Usain Bolt. Can you imagine any of these sports men and women in their prime just turning up to take part in their event/match? In the arts, would actress Katherine Hepburn, opera star Placido Domingo, popstar Madonna, or ballet dancer Rudolf Nureyev, just turn up on the day of the performance? They wouldn't dream of it – even the Rolling Stones practice.

So, if these people commit time and effort to practice, striving for perfection, to be the best they can be, what about the rest of us? Well, you will be familiar with the idea of exercise or going to the gym to achieve the fitness or physique you want. Practice is not just for elite performers. But what about the way you behave? Generally, people are constantly busy and "doing" (see Chapter 2 *Why*) and, for whatever reason, consciously or subconsciously end up being carried along on a wave of busyness rather than making conscious decisions about how, and who, they choose to be.

There is little focus on conscious practice and a lack of focus on reflection – on learning from that practice, considering what worked, what didn't work and what to adjust next time.

And this is about more than physical skills and actions, it is also about inner beliefs, ideas and attitudes.

"The mind is what separates a fair player from a true champion."
Kirk Mango[v]

WHAT DOES PRACTICE DO FOR YOU?

Practice helps you to deepen your knowledge, develop insight and broaden your capability. Science is providing increasing evidence that your brain is malleable and continually changing in response to your lifestyle, physiology and environment. Purposeful practice builds new neural pathways and constant repetition deepens those connections – the point is, you can have much more control over your mind, body and brain than you might think.

The result of all this practice? The seemingly super-sharp reaction time of various ball sports is an illusion. In standard reaction-time tests, there is no difference between, say, a leading tennis player compared to people in general. But, the player is able to detect minute subtle movement in the server's arm and shoulder and years of practice has led them to be able to read the direction of the serve before the ball has even been played. It's this practice that has created unconscious patterns and distinctions that the player responds to equally unconsciously – resulting in the seemingly super-sharp responses in the professional game.

Canadian Wayne Gretzky has been described as the greatest ice hockey player ever by many in his field. His talent is described in the context of a game rather than focusing on distinct skills alone. *"Gretzky's gift ... is for seeing ... amid the mayhem, Gretzky can discern the game's underlying pattern and flow, and anticipate what's going to happen faster and in more detail than anyone else."*[vi]

The same is said about experts in many fields. They instinctively know – based on years of practice. They are able to pick up minute distinctions and patterns that the rest of us are blind to.

> *"The more I practice, the luckier I get."*
> *Gary Player*[vii]

The story of a Cleveland firefighter, shared by Malcolm Gladwell.[viii]

The fire was in a kitchen in the back of a one-storey house in a residential neighbourhood. On breaking down the door, the firefighters began dousing the fire with water. It should have abated, but it did not.

The fire lieutenant suddenly thought to himself, *"There's something wrong here."* He immediately ordered his men out. Moments later, the floor they had been standing on collapsed. The fire had been in the basement, not the kitchen.

When asked how he knew to get out, the fireman could not immediately explain the reasons – the implicit knowledge, built up over years of experience, triggered an almost instinctive reaction, which saved his life and those of his crew members.

Purposeful practice is the primary contributing factor, above natural talent, to excellence in sport and life.[ix] To reach your peak performance in a skill or habit, hours of sustained practice are required – estimated at 10,000 hours (2.7 hours a day for 10 years).[x] This finding has been validated across professions. The focus and attention to the practice and learning from that practice is fundamental.

At this level of competence in a particular skills context, you have developed what is described as "reflection-in-action". This is where you are critically aware of what you are doing while you are doing it. You are judging each moment for its suitability against an inner set of criteria at the same time you are doing the activity.[xi] It's this attention to practice that enables you to keep performing at your best.

"It's not necessarily the amount of time you spend at practice that counts; it's what you put into the practice."
Eric Lindros[xii]

HUNGER FOR INFORMATION

Whatever you want to improve, begin by searching for information and insights from anywhere you can think of. You can learn from people you know, and the very best experts in the world. You may already use the internet to do this and, in particular, there has been an explosion of informative video clips to help you learn.

When watching these experts, paying attention to detail will help you to learn more. Have you ever taken the time to admire a skilled sportsperson, window cleaner, waiter or musician at work? Carefully watch what they are doing and the way they are doing it. What can you learn from them that you can practice? (see more about modelling in Chapter 15 *NLP*).

"When you are not practicing, remember, someone somewhere is practicing, and when you meet him he will win."
Ed Macauley[xiii]

PRACTICE AT PLAY

Whatever you choose to practice, treating this as "play" rather than "work," makes for a much more enjoyable experience. Play is simply applying what you have learned. And a play mindset casts a whole new light. There's no need to feel uncomfortable, vulnerable or exposed. When you do something for the first time, it is normal for it to feel clunky and unnatural. If you have learned how to serve in tennis and can remember your first attempts, you will know what we mean. Through practice, you are making the unfamiliar familiar.

A play mindset also makes failure easier to cope with, and failure is a key part of success (see Chapter 17 *Presuppositions*). It is relatively well known that inventor Thomas Edison "failed" many times before he had success with a light bulb. One story is that a young reporter came to interview him when he had tried more than 5,000 different filaments with no success. The young reporter asked: "Mr Edison, what is it like to have failed over 5,000 times?" To which Mr. Edison replied: "Young man, I haven't failed at all. I've succeeded at identifying 5,000 ways that don't work!" Edison's drive wasn't diminished at all. He continued and made more "mistakes" before he finally succeeded in creating the first filament light bulb.

Finally, a play mindset lifts self-imposed restrictions and boundaries. What would happen if you tried to juggle with four balls not three? The worst that can happen is that you drop the balls. You know other people can do it, so why shouldn't you be able to – with enough practice?

LEARNING THROUGH PRACTICE

How do you learn through practice?

Practicing something new takes you into a four-stage learning and performance cycle.[xiv]

Stage 1 – unconscious incompetence where you don't know what you don't know; ignorant bliss.

Stage 2 – conscious incompetence where you know what you don't know and are often acutely aware of your inability.

Stage 3 – conscious competence where you know how to perform the skill but need to focus to do it.

Stage 4 – unconscious competence where you don't know what you know and you perform the skill without conscious effort.

A fifth stage to this model has been described as developing reflection-in-action, where you consciously practice ongoing critical reflection. Building this reflective competence is something that can support you to build mastery.[xv]

"Practice is the best of all instructors."
Publilius Syrus[xvi]

HEART, MIND AND BODY

As you build new physical skills, you're laying down and deepening neural pathways. As you develop competence and strength in a particular skill, you're building up the positive emotions associated with execution. Practice in something can lead to belief in your ability to do it. This principle is one that informs coaches and practitioners working in the area of somatics and embodiment.

So if you embody confidence, in how you stand, walk, and engage with others, you will believe that you are confident. To put this to the test, try this simple experiment: Smile for fifteen seconds, then consider how you feel. The evidence all points towards smiling as a "cause" of happy feelings[xvii] not just a "result" of happy feelings (see Chapter 17 *Presuppositions*).

AND STILL YOU MIGHT NOT KNOW

There will also be times when you will never know the impact of your practice. A colleague of ours attended a workshop focused on the value of "compassion". On her way home that evening she passed a beggar at the train station and because the topic was still front of mind, she decided to put into practice what had been discussed at the workshop and gave him three pounds. What happened next took her by surprise. He said, "Can you make it a fiver?" which caused her to say, "No, I cannot," in a curt manner before rushing off, questioning the gesture she had made. Let's consider this for a moment though. Sometimes you will have a good intention but things may not turn out the way you wanted or expected. The key is to maintain resilience and follow what is important to you. And besides, who's to say the beggar did not reflect on the situation, his behaviour, our colleague's reaction, and realized something that then changed his behaviour the next time. Only he will ever know.

PRACTICE
and my31Practices

The my31Practices approach is about putting your values into practice every day. Being aware of your personal values is an important first step – but, on its own, this is not enough. To be "lived", and the way of being, the values have to be practiced.

Because there is a myPractice each day, you have the chance to practice one behaviour which is directly related to one of the core values. For example, you may have the core value "compassion", and a myPractice to bring this value to life, "I offer help to strangers who look in need". On the day of this particular myPractice, you are therefore very mindful and consciously looking for opportunities to offer help to a stranger. The impact? Let's consider:

Over the course of one month, you live each of your values through a number of different myPractices. Initially, like any new activity, you may feel uncertain, awkward and even a little anxious: "Am I doing it right?" "What will people think of me?" Over time the myPractices are repeated, becoming habitual (see Chapter 11 *Habit*) – you don't have to think about them and they become automatic. You have your focus for the day and you can also take opportunities to practice your other myPractices. There are no restrictions.

Repeated "purposeful practice" of behaviours and attitudes that are explicitly linked to your core values will result in you mastering your values.

PRACTICE
- in practice

Practice deliberate practice. This could be something like juggling, repeating some phrases in a foreign language or one simple piece on a musical instrument. If you want something easier, practice asking the servers in a shop, restaurant or coffee shop how they are. Notice how you feel and how your performance improves.

PAUSE FOR THOUGHT...

What difference could practice make to any one small part
of your life?

WANT TO KNOW MORE?

http://www.my31practices.com/the-book/resources/chapter-12

REINFORCEMENT

*"There are two things people want
more than sex and money –
recognition and praise."*
Mary Kay Ash[i]

Rewards work wonders for dogs. They work for people too – including you. Many of you will be familiar with physiologist Ivan Pavlov's work with dogs and their conditioned response to a bell ringing.[ii] But it was behavioural psychologist B F Skinner who first demonstrated instrumental reinforcement and the many ways it works in everyday life, not just in animals but in humans as well.[iii] In his theory of Operant Conditioning, Skinner performed a number of experiments that proved behaviour could be taught through giving rewards. Positive reinforcement as a consequence to an action increases the likelihood that action will happen again. These "rewards" are called "positive reinforcers" and are an important part of motivation[iv] (also see Chapter 10 *Habit*).

Positive reinforcement is a simple technique that can help to change behaviour, sometimes surprisingly quickly, if implemented properly. It takes more effort – you know how easy it is to spot something wrong and be critical of things that are not right, but this "reward" is the most important part of forming a habit.[v] The approach is just as relevant to yourself as for other people – you can reinforce and reward your own good decisions – and the power of gratitude is increasingly recognized.[vi]

Reinforcement works best when it takes place immediately after an action, to make a strong connection between the two. The positive reinforcement, or "reward" itself, can take a whole range of different forms. In the world of employee engagement, rewards can be divided into four categories: transactional, relational, individual and communal.[vii] Transactional rewards are tangible whereas relational rewards are intangible and, perhaps obviously, individual rewards are for one person, whereas communal rewards are group or community based. A reward can fit with more than one category, e.g. transactional individual. Here are some examples using these categories. Have a go at working out the categories the following rewards fit into:

Personal objectives bonus

– ....

Team achievement certificate

– ....

A hand-written note to thank a member of the team

– ....

Employee survey

– ....

These reinforcers work for most people, but what works well for one person on one occasion may not reinforce somebody else – or even the same person on another occasion.

The more personal and relevant or "in the moment" it can be, the more effective it is: something that is really appreciated at a personal level, immediately. This may sometimes take a while to identify and to do, but, in our experience, is worth the extra effort.

> *"The way positive reinforcement is carried out is more important than the amount."*
> B F Skinner

POSITIVE IMPACT

Positive reinforcement can be very powerful. It creates an environment of encouragement and praise instead of criticism, and this creates good feelings, builds self-esteem, confidence and independence, and builds a culture of trust. The focus on taking positive action means there is less time for unproductive and potentially stressful discussion or thought about unwanted behaviour. It also motivates people, individually and collectively, to continue with similar actions, thus creating a virtuous circle. Finally, it can help people to identify and make the best use of their strengths to achieve more.

JUST A MINUTE

If, from what you have read so far, you are thinking the topic of positive reinforcement is a straightforward one, we owe you an apology. At one level, it is a simple concept, but delve deeper and it is full of complexity.

Consistency is an example of this. On the one hand, you might think that a particular behaviour which is considered positive or desirable, and which has been rewarded in the past, should continue to be rewarded over time. If this does not happen, there is a risk of confusion and indecisiveness about repeating the behaviour in future. On the other hand, you might have noticed when somebody has been praised for something it has a major positive effect. However, after several repetitions, the praise can become an expectation and therefore loses some of its reinforcing value.

Intermittent reinforcement is the off-and-on use of rewards, and it is very effective in locking in behaviours. By reducing the frequency of the reinforcement, the desired behaviour will actually occur more consistently. Dr Skinner mapped out schedules of reinforcement in thousands of studies, showing how the strength of reinforcement changed as a function of how often the reinforcing occurred.

There is even a case that can be made for unearned rewards having a positive impact as demonstrated by the Parable of the Porpoise,[viii] where porpoises were given fish as a method to encourage them to perform new behaviours.

We trust that this chapter has given you some thoughts and ideas to ponder but, ultimately, there is no substitute for practicing a range of methods and techniques, as different people have different preferences in different situations.

REINFORCEMENT
and my31Practices

Reinforcement is a core foundation of the my31Practices approach and you can use a number of different features to support you. The different types of reinforcement mentioned earlier are built in to the my31Practices approach:

- Transactional – scoring or rating your performance at the end of the day
- Relational – the whole essence of my31Practices is about strengthening the relationship with yourself
- Individual – everything is focused on recognizing "your" successes and areas for development
- Communal – sharing your myExperiences with colleagues and friends

One of the features of my31Practices we enjoy most is choosing a quote, a picture and a video that reinforces the message of the myPractice. Thinking of the value of "success", you might choose the quote "What gets measured, gets done", the Beatles song "It's getting better all the time", and a photo of Usain Bolt winning a gold medal. The great thing is that you choose the quotes, pictures and video clips that resonate strongly with you and so, by definition, they motivate you. Developments in neuroscience and specifically neurofeedback are creating a better understanding of this area.[ix] You can spend a few minutes at the beginning of the day looking at these "reinforcers" and consciously set yourself up for the day with your myPractice at the front of your mind (see Chapter 7 *Mindfulness*).

Another important area of reinforcement is "reward", and with my31Practices this happens immediately when you do something in line with your myPractice – you feel a sense of achievement straight away.

Then, at the end of each day, you receive a reminder to think about your myPractice – what you have done well and what you could have done better. It is up to you to what extent you use quantitative or qualitative measurement (see Chapter 14 *Assessment*) and both options are available. You can rate your performance and/or make a few notes of the myExperiences and what the impact was on other people and yourself.

Rating and recording the experiences helps in a number of ways: it is a reward in itself because it gives you a sense of achievement and completion, it reinforces your behaviour for the day itself, and also builds a "catalogue" of experiences to demonstrate the cumulative impact of your series of small actions. You can also set up a reward at the end of the month according to your average score. Nobody will check up on you though, so you might as well be honest with yourself! At the same time, there is no obligation to use any of these reward/recognition features. Some people are less comfortable with the idea of self-reward and if this is you, why not just give it a try or, rather than reward yourself, give something to somebody else?

REINFORCEMENT
- in practice

Think of a behaviour you would like to display. Start with something small and not too challenging. Use one or more of the positive reinforcement techniques above and see what impact this has. Pay attention to what works well for you, and what works less well.

The answers to the questions about motivation are:

- Personal objectives bonus – transactional individual
- Team achievement certificate – transactional communal
- A hand written note to thank a member of the team – relational individual
- Employee survey – relational communal

PAUSE FOR THOUGHT ...

How did you feel the last time somebody recognized your efforts?

WANT TO KNOW MORE?

http://www.my31practices.com/the-book/resources/chapter-13

ASSESSMENT

"I made my own assessment of my life, and I began to live it. That was freedom."
Fernando Flores[i]

Do you remember receiving gold stars at primary school, being timed for a mile run, homework comments, exams and grades, and then later on trials or selection for a representative team, going on a date, taking your driving test, job interviews, receiving a flat/room inspection, a health check-up, performance reviews, your Grand Theft Auto[ii] points score, or just recently looking at your "to do" list? From an early age, performance assessment and measurement become an integral part of your life. This will continue as technology makes it easier to capture and display data, and mobile phones and apps have played a big part. Did you know that sales of smart wearables are expected to grow from 9.7 million in 2013 to 135 million in 2018?[iii] These devices are being used in areas such as nutrition, fitness, wellbeing, etc, and perhaps this is an opportunity for further development of www.my31Practices.com.

One of our favourite stories demonstrating the power of the simple act of measurement is about a steel-making plant. The president of the plant liked to tour the building daily. During one inspection he came across a group of employees who had just finished pouring ingot. The president quickly counted the ingots and without saying anything wrote 78 in bold figures with a piece of chalk. Then he continued his tour. When he came to the same station the next day, 78 had been crossed through and beside it his employees had written 80. One day later, 80 was crossed out and replaced with 85. Production continued to increase in this manner.[iv]

"When performance is measured, performance improves.
When performance is measured and reported back,
the rate of improvement accelerates."
Thomas S Monson[v]

At a conceptual level, the benefits of measurement seem obvious. If people are accountable for their performance, which is then assessed by a system of measurement, judgments can be made and decisions can be taken – for example, good performance can be rewarded and under-performance addressed.

"Measurement is the first step that leads to control and
eventually to improvement. If you can't measure something,
you can't understand it. If you can't understand it, you can't
control it. If you can't control it, you can't improve it."
H James Harrington[vi]

The benefits of using measurement are reinforced by empirical findings in the psychological literature on goal setting (see Chapter 22 *Goals*).[vii] But not everybody has the same point of view. Detractors stress the costs and potential for dysfunction associated with measurement in organizations.

You can probably think of your own examples where measurement in organizations does not add much value. Two of our favourites (which might be urban myths) where the outcome is totally counterproductive are:

Example 1: A call centre put in place a bonus payment scheme for employees to try to ensure phones were being answered quickly. After a short time, management was confused because, while the bonuses were being paid out, there were lots of customer complaints. Investigation revealed that the call handlers were cutting off callers mid-conversation to answer new calls to hit the targets.

Example 2: A bus company incentivized drivers to be on time for at least 90% of the route stops. The result? When some drivers were running late, they missed stops to make up time. Just picture the amazement on the faces of the people waiting as the bus drove right past.

In other cases, the measurement system can create an industry and seems to become an end in itself. People become a slave to the system, seemingly oblivious to why measurement was introduced in the first place.

W Edwards Deming, often considered the father of both the Japanese and the American quality movements, has declared performance measurement, *"the most powerful inhibitor to quality and productivity in the western world".*[viii]

In support of Deming's quote, this story is from a project providing office services (reception, catering, security, cleaning, meeting rooms, helpdesk, etc.) to a client's new building in London:

There was discussion about performance targets. The client wanted to see an improvement in a helpdesk's results being achieved in other offices. They wanted to have targets which were realistic and achievable. It was suggested that there should not be any targets for the first year of operation and, instead, everybody would be encouraged to perform to the best of their ability. The results achieved in that first year were not only better than the other established offices, they far exceeded what the client thought would be possible. This is a great example of how measurement can create a limiting mindset – watch out, you get what you ask for.[ix]

Our conclusion is that assessment or measurement on its own is not a driver of performance. In the steel-making plant above, it is likely that there were other things happening which motivated the employees. Extrinsic and intrinsic motivation are both important ways of driving behaviour.[x] It is important to understand some of the key differences between the two types of motivation and how they can be best used, particularly the overall impact that each can have on behaviour.

We like this concise summary from social psychologist David G. Myers:[xi]

"A person's interest often survives when a reward is used neither to bribe nor to control, but to signal a job well done, as in a "most improved player" award. If a reward boosts your feeling of competence after doing good work, your enjoyment of the task might increase. Rewards, rightly administered, can motivate high performance and creativity. And extrinsic rewards (such as scholarships, admissions, and jobs that often follow good grades) are here to stay."

In our experience of leading people-based organizations, a focus on intrinsic motivation (but not at the exclusion of extrinsic motivators), combined with measurement-based recognition, is a highly effective approach, and these principles are built into the way www.my31Practices.com works. We also recognize that people are not all the same, and this is why my31Practices has a couple of different assessment and measurement functions to choose from.

ASSESSMENT
and my31Practices

Assessment with my31Practices works in two ways:

From a quantitative perspective, you can give yourself a simple score at the end of each day to assess how well you think you have lived your myPractice. You can see your cumulative performance for the month and, if you want to, can also set rewards against your monthly score. The important thing is to remember why you are doing the scoring. It is not to achieve a high score. Instead, it is to give you a sense of how you are performing and where you could do better, and to help you identify and consider trends and themes. Why do you regularly score highly on one particular myPractice but not on another? The score itself is not so important and, after all, nobody is going to check! You can award six stars if you want to, but who will you be fooling and how would this help you? It might be helpful to share your scores with friends or people who share similar values to you, to act as motivation. You can do this by email or on social media such as Twitter and Facebook.

From a qualitative perspective, you are prompted to record your myExperience from the day, which encourages personal reflection – or in other words assessment! You might have read in Chapter 13 *Reinforcement* how this is a mini-reward in itself, because it is confirmation of your achievement of practicing your myPractice. It is also a way to "capture" the memory which may otherwise be lost among everything else that has happened in a busy day.

Finally, the act of recalling the situation and recording it in some detail helps to further reinforce the neural pathways, increasing the likelihood of repeated behaviour. The result is a great example of effective experiential learning (see Chapter 10 *Learning*).

> *"Not everything that can be counted counts, and not everything that counts can be counted."*
> *William Bruce Cameron[xii]*

You might be wondering which of these two approaches is more effective, and there is probably no clear-cut answer, because people are different. We prefer to think "and", rather than "or", so why don't you try both the qualitative and quantitative approaches and see what works for you?

PAUSE FOR THOUGHT ...

How do you assess the way you behave and how this fits with "being you"?

WANT TO KNOW MORE?

http://www.my31practices.com/the-book/resources/chapter-14

PART 3
NLP

Part 3 is an exploration of the practical elements of my31 Practices and provides some useful information, tools and strategies to help you implement my31Practices. This section also explains why it all works, through a neuro-linguistic programming (NLP) lens. Its purpose is to enable you to develop your insight into how and why the my31Practices approach works from a human per-spective. We explore a number of topics and continue with additional exercises and signposting to further resources. Part 3 is designed to support Part 2, but it isn't essential to have read it to work with my31Practices in your daily life.

We have organized this section into the following chapters: Chapter 15 *NLP* is a summary exploration of the NLP approach; Chapter 16 *Maps* demonstrates how we create our versions of reality; Chapter 17 *Presuppositions* explores the concept of assumed truths and their impact; Chapter 18 *Awareness* shares how we can become more aware of ourselves and others; Chapter 19 *Alignment* looks at a process for making sure our choices are aligned; Chapter 20 *Beliefs* examines the importance and impact of beliefs on performance; Chapter 21 *mBIT* highlights an entirely new field in NLP coaching that aligns head, heart and gut; and Chapter 22 *Goals* looks at some simple, yet powerful, processes for successful goal setting. However, you will notice a lot of overlap and connection between these chapters because many of them are part of each other. We suggest that you read Chapter 15 *NLP* and Chapter 16 *Maps* first and then feel free to start with a subject that you are most attracted to and follow your interests from there.

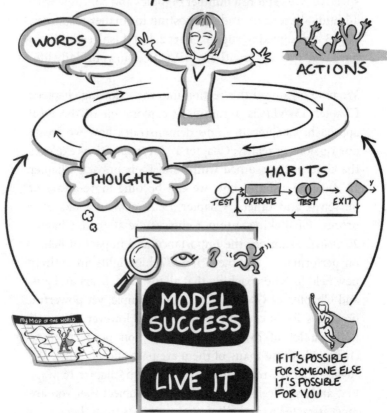

*"Watch your **thoughts**, they become your words,*
*Watch your **words**, they become your actions,*
*Watch your **actions**, they become your habits,*
*Watch your **habits**, they become your destiny."*
Lao Tzu[i]

Here's what might appear to be an obvious statement: If you don't like what you're doing and the results you are getting, do something different.

Perhaps that might sound too simple, maybe even easier said than done. Given the right motivation, tools and strategies, this can become a far simpler process than you might at first think. Welcome to the world of neuro-linguistic programming (NLP).

The principles of NLP complement the my31Practices approach perfectly because, at the simplest level, they focus on how you think, act and get results. You can use many of the NLP tools, techniques and strategies to help you make the my31Practices approach work for you to achieve the results you want.

Part of the NLP toolkit includes understanding the role "values" play in your life. As my31Practices is about releasing the power of your personal values to be the best you can be – your best YOU – it is clear to us that there is great synergy between the two.

So, what is NLP? NLP is a systematic process for understanding and influencing the connection between your thoughts, words, actions and reactions.

As we begin to explore NLP a little more, it might be useful to understand just what the title means from a neuro-linguistic programming perspective:

Neuro: The mind and how you use neurological filtering to process information from your five senses and create your experience.
Linguistic: How you assign language to give your filtered experience meaning.
Programming: Your behavioural patterns based on the above; in other words, your habits.

NLP has been described in some quarters as " the ultimate behavioural engineering tool."[ii] It has also been described as the "art and science of personal excellence,"[iii] an art because you bring your own creativity to it, your own "X" factor if you like; and science because it follows a methodology, a process for uncovering excellence and then replicating it. This process is known as modelling.

ORIGINS

NLP was developed in the early 1970s when Richard Bandler, a psychology student at the University of California, Santa Cruz, and John Grinder, an associate professor of linguistics at the university, studied three very effective therapists: father of Gestalt therapy, Fritz Perls; family therapist Virginia Satir; and world renowned hypnotherapist, Milton H Erickson.[iv].

The key question for Bandler and Grinder was to identify the differences between people who excel at what they do, and other people who are merely average at the same thing. They showed that it was possible to model the effective patterns of these three therapists to create a "code", and then give that code to other people so that they could achieve the same or similar results.

MODELLING

At its simplest form, NLP is modelling, or copying the strategies of people who excel in what they do in a given context. Grinder describes the modelling process as the *"mapping of tacit knowledge onto an explicit model,"*[v] that is making available the set of key differences that lead to excellent results. In one way, the awareness of what is often tacit knowledge (values[vi]) and mapping that onto an explicit model (behaviours), is what the my31Practices approach does.

Modelling is one of the most effective ways in which you can learn and pick up new skills. You have been modelling in this way since you first came into the world; for example, you learned to speak your native language by unconsciously copying those around you. Through a series of constant feedback loops, you refined the process until you could speak fluently.

UNCONSCIOUS ASSIMILATION

"Just Do It."
Nike[vii]

The modelling process of seeing or hearing someone do something that works and then repeating the behaviour to see what results you get, is known as unconscious assimilation in NLP. You may notice that a new behaviour works from the sensory feedback you receive, it just "feels" right. This can be experienced when learning a new language with a native speaker and simply repeating something they have said and sensing that it fits the context and is appropriate. This works well when you do not filter your response by feeling embarrassed, you simply "do". The Nike "just do it" brand campaign comes to mind here as a great example. When we apply more formal, conscious-minded strategies, such as learning grammar in a classroom, it can take us longer. Add to that the filter of being embarrassed to make mistakes, and the process can be stretched out even further.

"Lose your mind and come to your senses."
Fritz Perls[viii]

As a note, this process of feeling embarrassed has a logical structure to it involving our belief systems, which we explore further in Chapter 20 *Beliefs*.

APPLICATIONS

Essentially, NLP practitioners are pattern detectives, seeking out the patterns we run in our lives. In your life, for example, you will be running some patterns that help you achieve and others that hold you back or make things a little more challenging. These patterns are habits. In various contexts of your life, NLP processes can help you to reinforce patterns that serve you and change patterns that do not serve you:

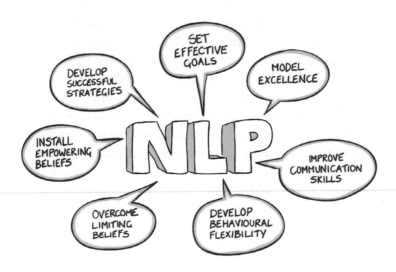

Figure 5. NLP Applications

SUBJECTIVE REALITY

NLP master trainers and authors Robert Dilts and Judith DeLozier describe NLP as; *"the study of the structure of subjective experience."*[ix] This definition highlights an important point: that you interpret your experiences subjectively based on a personal and unique set of filters. By way of example, you might notice that some people do not always see things the way you do. This is because we all filter our experiences differently (see Chapter 16 *Maps*).

Imagine several people watching a film at the cinema, some people may love the film, some hate it and some may be ambivalent. They might have shared the same experience, but how they interpret that experience is entirely subjective.

You might have heard the expression: "There is your point of view, the other person's point of view, and somewhere in the middle, the truth". The ability to change the way you look at something is crucial to developing behavioural flexibility and increasing personal choice. Take the hypothetical situation of a colleague who turns up late for work. You may believe that means they do not care about what they do, and that could affect the way you feel about them. However, is the meaning that you assigned to their behaviour the "truth", or just one of many possible interpretations? What if you later discover that the reason they were late was because they had stopped to help someone who had been involved in an accident? How would you feel then? Perhaps your version, or "map", of reality might change.

If your maps are formed from your interpretation of events, and there can be many different valid interpretations, how useful would it be to actively interpret events in a way that empowers you, rather than limits you?

Fortunately, NLP offers a range of practical and accessible tools for you to influence your maps and bring about positive change, in order to lead a life more aligned with what is important to you. This makes for great synergy with the my31Practices approach.

YOU ARE IN CHARGE OF YOUR MIND

Human beings are complex creatures and we are discovering more and more from recent advances in the study of neuroscience about the way we function. One of the key NLP foundation stones (see Chapter 17 *Presuppositions*) is that the mind and body is a linked system,[x] and there is research that indicates this to be true. Your mental attitude will affect you physically, including having an effect on your health[xi]. There is a link between stress levels and disease in the body, for example.[xii]

Another developing area of science is how our thinking, decisions, and actions are influenced sometimes by our head "brain", sometimes by our heart "brain",[xiii] and sometimes our gut "brain" (see Chapter 21 *mBIT*). Having an awareness of this can help you find balance when head, heart, and gut appear to be in conflict.

CORE SKILLS

There is a set of skills that form the basis of all NLP processes. These include:

- Awareness and calibration (see Chapter 18 *Awareness*): The ability to detect changes in you and others.
- Rapport: The ability to resonate with your environment, including with yourself and others. Rapport is unconscious responsiveness; it is connecting and resonating at the same frequency as others. Rapport is essential for building an environment of trust between people.
- Triple positioning (see Chapter 18 *Awareness*): Seeing things from multiple perspectives.
- Language: The words we use not only influence others but also reveal our own processing and belief systems.

THE PRINCIPLES OF SUCCESS

NLP has a simple structure to help achieve successful outcomes. This structure comprises of a number of key steps:

1. Know your outcome

> *"Know what you want to do, hold the thought firmly,*
> *and do every day what should be done, and every*
> *sunset will see you that much nearer to your goal."*
> *Elbert Hubbard* [xiv]

Know what it is you are looking to achieve. Be very clear and unambiguous about this. Well-defined outcomes will help you to know how best to move towards them. In addition, your chance of achieving an outcome works best when you state it as a positive you want to move towards, for example, "I want to buy a house", rather than a negative you want to move away from, "I don't want to rent a property any more". Imagine saying to a taxi driver, "I don't want to go to JFK airport, I don't want to go to Times Square, and I don't want to go to Central Park." The driver cannot take you anywhere until you have established where you want to go. These principles are applied to how your write your myPractices in Chapter 9 *Affirmation*.

2. Have excellent awareness

> *"You manage what you measure."*
> *Gretchen Rubin*[xv]

Most successful strategies involve the ability to be aware of how you are progressing towards what you want. If you have a budget of £300 each month, you might want to set weekly targets to know if you are on track. It would not be good to discover that you have spent the £300 with one week left to go. This principle is covered in Chapter 14 *Assessment*.

3. Be flexible

"The measure of intelligence is the ability to change."
Albert Einstein[xvi]

A key to success is the principle that if what you are doing is not working, or stops working, do something else. Repeating unsuccessful patterns in the same context will inevitably lead to unsuccessful outcomes. This is the reason why your myPractices are more effective when they are written in such a way that they are specific enough for you to know if you have practiced them or not, but general enough to give you the flexibility to apply them in an appropriate way to a variety of activities.

4. Operate from a physiology and psychology of excellence

"If you are going to achieve excellence in big things, you develop the habit in little matters. Excellence is not an exception, it is a prevailing attitude."
Colin Powell[xvii]

The mind and body are a linked system. If you walk around with your shoulders hunched, head down looking at the floor, you are likely to experience negative emotions and low energy. If you are telling yourself that something is impossible, you may well be making that true for yourself. Experience what happens when your physiology is more empowering, your thoughts also. Feel the difference when you tell yourself that your task is possible, that you can do it, that you will do it. See what a difference this can make to both motivation and results. Look around at people you know who are successful. Notice how they carry themselves, and listen to what they say. They are using empowering psychophysical patterns. By practicing your myPractices you will be embedding your own empowering' habits, thoughts and feelings aligned to what is most important to you, your personal values.

5. Build and maintain rapport

> *"Treasure your relationships, not your possessions."*
> *Anthony J D'Angelo*

The more you can connect and resonate with those around you, the greater your chance of positively influencing them, assisting them, and having them want to assist you in whatever you are doing. One way in which my31Practices supports this is consistency of intention and behaviour, using your values to guide your decisions, choices and actions.

6. Take Action!

> *"Do you want to know who you are? Don't ask. Act!*
> *Action will delineate and define you."*
> *Thomas Jefferson[xix]*

It doesn't matter how often you talk about your plans, dreams and aspirations if you do not take steps towards what you want. Can you think of people you know who are always talking about what they are going to do one day? Walk your talk! The my31Practices approach is all about taking small actions every day.

Ecology

In NLP, ecology is defined as the study of consequences, and all change should be evaluated in terms of context and ecology. Since NLP and my31Practices are about personal change, it is essential to consider what potential consequences these changes may bring to yourself, others and the larger system in which you exist.

Here are some simple questions you can use to check the ecology of an intended change:

- What are the positive outcomes that are likely to happen if you make this change?
- What are the negative outcomes that are likely to happen if you make this change?
- What happens if you do not make this change?
- What doesn't happen if you make this change?
- What doesn't happen if you don't make this change? (Bear with this question; it is designed to make you think!)

A question that is designed to test motivation and/or potential barriers to change could be: "As a percentage, how much do you want to make this change?" If the answer to this question is not 100%, for example 95%, it is worth asking: "What is that other 5% about?"

In summary, NLP is a systemic approach involving strategies that enable you to achieve what you want by influencing the relationship between your thoughts, feelings, words and actions. It uses many reframing techniques and processes to give your past and present experiences meanings that empower you and take you towards what you want. NLP also helps you model successful patterns and replicate them to give you the best chance of reaching desired outcomes. These tools are very powerful and should always be used ecologically, taking into consideration the consequences surrounding any change you intend to make.

PAUSE FOR THOUGHT ...

From what you know so far, what three aspects of NLP do you believe will bring you most benefit?

WANT TO KNOW MORE?

http://www.my31practices.com/the-book/resources/chapter-15

MAPS

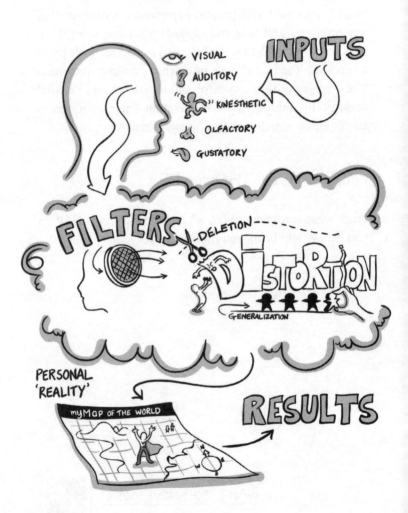

"Change the way you look at things and
the things you look at change."
Wayne W Dyer[i]

A map is a representation of something; it is not the thing it represents. A map of a town might show the road layout, where buildings, fields and parks are, but it is not the bricks and mortar; it is not the green grass or the asphalt on the road, with its various potholes and cracks.

You create internal maps from your external experience. What you pick up through your five senses is translated into what you perceive.

"If there were no difference between appearance and reality,
then there would be no need for science."
Karl Marx[ii]

In reality, what can be measured with science, might be quite different from what you actually perceive, and very different from the meaning you might give it. For example, you might see an oak table and perceive it as a solid, fixed mass. Science, however, tells us that the table is actually made of millions of moving particles, so perception and reality already differ. If you then decide that the table is beautiful, this is based on your personal filters and interpretation – your "map" of reality.

Generally therefore you are not limited or empowered by reality, but rather by your map of that reality.[iii]

An understanding of how you create your maps can be empowering. Through becoming aware of the filters you use to create meaning, you can begin the process of changing those filters. You might come to view previous "assumed" constraints as limiting beliefs you no longer hold on to. Wouldn't that be great?

Can you recall a time when you have believed that something held you back, only to later change your point of view completely?

Imagine a scenario where your best friend doesn't call when they said they would. You are upset and don't speak to them for a week. You might later discover that they had been ill and unable to call you. Your immediate reaction was based on the assumption that your best friend didn't care enough about you to call. Later, you realized that this was not the case – it was simply an illusion you had created. How often do you operate under such illusions?

Alternatively, you might also operate under assumptions that serve you and make you more effective. These kinds of assumptions are also known as empowering beliefs. You might view meeting people at a party as an opportunity to make new friends, for example, as opposed to feeling a sense of inadequacy through comparing yourself to others.

PERCEPTION AND MEANING

So, why is it that when somebody else interprets a certain action as a sign of weakness, you might interpret the same action as a sign of strength?

The NLP Communication Model explains the process by which we create meaning from an experience. The model is also referred to as NLP Epistemology:[iv] the study of how we know what we know.

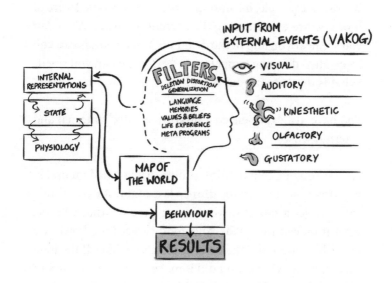

Figure 6. The NLP Communication Model

HOW WE CREATE OUR "MAPS"

Input

Assuming there are no neurological issues, you experience the outside world through your senses of sight, sound, touch or feel, smell and taste. NLP refers to the five senses as VAKOG: **v**isual (sight), **a**uditory (sound), **k**inesthetic (touch/feel), **o**lfactory (smell) and **g**ustatory (taste). Also, see Chapter 10 *Learning*.

By way of example, look around you now. Become aware of how you are experiencing the present moment. What can you see near you and in the distance? What sounds can you hear? How does the temperature feel? What can you smell? What is the taste in your mouth?

You have just experienced a mixture of "live" internal and external senses.

Now take a moment to think about what you had for breakfast this morning, or for dinner last night. As you think, can you get a visual in your mind's eye of what you ate, what it looked like? Was your food served in a bowl or a plate? If so, what did the bowl or plate look like? If the food was crunchy, what sound did it make when you chewed it? What did it smell like? What did it taste like?

In order to recall these past events, you use the same five senses as you did a moment ago when you looked around you.

The five senses that you use to experience the world and then re-present past events, as memories or recollections, are known as the representational systems in NLP. You also use the same representational systems to imagine what the future could be like (see Chapter 22 *Goals*). In fact, your entire life experience is coded in representational systems.

Figure 6, The NLP Communication Model (page 163) shows your five senses creating an internal version of what you experience on the outside. This is your "first access" to your internal "experience". What you perceive is the result of neurological transformations[v] that have acted upon the input from your five senses, for example, light waves have been translated into images, sound waves into what you hear, and so on. In other words your experience is made up of sights, sounds, feelings, smells and tastes.

Filters

Your first access experience is then filtered through various deletions, distortions and generalizations to create and define your interpretation of the experience, also known as your map.

When you looked around the room a moment ago, did you notice how you felt about being where you are? Did you think it was a good place to be, or not? Why did you think this? Are you aware of the process that led you to make that judgment?

When you thought about your breakfast or dinner, how did you feel about the food? Was it good, bad or were you indifferent? What led you to think that?

For you to make judgments on the above, you would have had to run your experiences through your unique filters.

Because your filters are unique to you, you will create different interpretations of an experience from others. Consider, for example, a rainy day. This might make one person feel miserable, and yet it might make you feel alive and want to fling open the doors and run around outside with open arms, feeling the fresh rain wash over you. These are very different interpretations of the fact that it is raining. It is these differences in filtering that make people so different and interesting. It is the reason we have different tastes in fashion, musical preferences, art, literature, and so on, and the reason we make different choices. It can also lead to conflict in the world. Different perspectives, beliefs and philosophies on life can lead to a desire to learn from each other or, at the opposite end of the spectrum, to do battle with each other.

Where do our filters come from? We develop them over time from influences such as our environment, parents, family, friends, life experience, school, media, role models and religion.

As shown in Figure 6, the type of filters we use to alter our experience may be categorized as deletion, distortion and generalization:[vi] These filters are important because there are so many bits of information hitting us every second[vii] that we would be overloaded if we did not have a system to make this information manageable.

Deletion

In 1956, the eminent psychologist, George A. Miller, postulated that we can only be aware of between five and nine chunks of information (see Chapter 18 *Awareness*). This is a small number, especially when you consider the amount of information bombarding us every second. Therefore we delete much of what is around us to be able to function. If we did not do this, we would fall into process overload.

To retain as much information as possible, we group bits of information together. Ask a few people to tell you their mobile phone number and listen to see how they have "chunked" the numbers into smaller groups to be able to remember them. How would you and your friends "chunk" this number 665172439852 to remember it?:

You:

Friend:

Let's look at another example of deletion. After you have read this sentence, close your eyes for 60 seconds and then describe where you are in as much detail as you can. Include everything in your immediate vicinity, such as the number of windows, what shape and size they are, their colour, or how many tables there are and what is on them, the colour of the carpet, or whatever is relevant. Do this right now and resist the temptation to peek! Thank you – now that you have opened your eyes, look around you. How much did you remember? And how much did you miss, or in other words, delete?

You cannot remember all that is around you. What you do recall largely depends on what your current intention is.

To explore this concept of intention, look at the passage in bold below. You may have come across this example before. We choose to use it here because it provides a great example of deletion. Give yourself 10 seconds to read the paragraph below and count how many "F"s are present in the text. Do not read below the passage until you have finished. Go!

FINISHED FILES ARE THE RESULT OF YEARS OF SCIENTIFIC STUDY COMBINED WITH THE EXPERIENCE OF MANY YEARS

How many did you count? The answer is in the illustration introducing this chapter. When we run this test in a classroom situation, there is always a mix of answers from three to six. If you used an auditory strategy in this task and were reading while listening for the sound "F", then you might well have missed a few "F"s that when pronounced sound like "V"s, as in the word "of". If you delete information from your experience when reading a passage of text in this way, imagine what you could be deleting in your day-to-day life.

Your intention directs your attention, which directs your awareness, and you respond to what you are aware of; in other words when you set your intentions, you set your filters.[viii] Because people have a different set of intentions from one another, you might notice and delete different things within a shared experience. As a result, two people can have different experiences of the same situation and circumstances (see Chapter 18 *Awareness*).

Distortion

A distortion is where you take an experience and make it mean something it is not. For example, if you see someone cross their arms, you might think that person is a "closed" person. However, it could also be that they are feeling chilly or that crossing their arms is comfortable for them. The distortion comes from assigning the meaning "closed" to the action of arm crossing when it could be for any one of a number of reasons. You might have used the expression "that is a distortion of the facts!"

A mind-read is a form of distortion. A mind-read is claiming to know what someone thinks without having any factual basis for the interpretation. It is actually no more than a guess that you believe to be true. For example, if you say something to someone and they frown, you might mind-read that as meaning that they do not agree with you. However, they could be thinking that you are right and their frown is a result of them questioning their own assumptions.

We also distort our memories. Have you ever visited your old primary school? Why does it seem so much smaller than you remembered?

Generalization

A generalization involves deleting the differences that make something unique, producing a generalized perception. This is demonstrated by an experiment[ix] where Person A approached people with the pretence of asking directions. When an unwitting participant had started giving directions, two "workmen" walked between them carrying a large sheet of plasterboard. The shield provided by the board was used to replace Person A with a replacement, Person B. The research measured whether the person giving directions noticed that they were now giving them to a totally different person. Amazingly, slightly less than half of the people approached noticed the switch. The person giving directions had not been aware of the specific individual; they had generalized "a person asking for directions".

Other generalizations may be experienced in the form of value judgments, for example, "English people are very polite", or "Australian people are very relaxed", or "American people are very ambitious", etc. There might be characteristics that some people share; however, these are not rules. We know people from the countries mentioned above who do not fit the stated generalizations!

EXAMPLE FILTERS

Here are three examples of how deletions, distortions and generalizations can affect the meaning you give to an experience.

Values: A value is something that is important to you and acts as a very strong filter. If one of your core values is to be on time and someone is late to meet you, this is likely to affect the way you respond to that person – you will probably not think well of them. Similarly, if you are asked to do something that goes against your values, you are likely to find it a challenge to carry out that task with full conviction or to the best of your ability.

For example, imagine that you are a salesperson and one of your core values is "honesty". You are asked to sell something to someone who does not need your product and you know they cannot afford it. This will probably make it difficult or impossible for you to make the sale. Your filter is telling you that the situation is wrong and this affects your behaviour. More generally, you may feel that this job is not for you.

Contrast this with someone who has a core value of "achievement", will do anything to succeed, and has no reservations in making the sale. They might consider this to be a great job.

Our internal filter of values influences our judgments of an experience.

Beliefs: A belief is a best guess or opinion, not a fact. Beliefs can help you (empowering beliefs) or they can hold you back (limiting beliefs). For example, if you are persuading somebody about something, you are likely to have more conviction and perform better if you believe in that something.

Life experience: If you go into a situation that is similar to one you have had before, you might find your approach to the new situation is influenced by the memory of the previous one. If you went for a job interview and it did not go very well, you might carry that memory into the next interview, which could affect your state. You might be nervous again, not based on the new interview but based on your previous experience.

At the same time, bringing past experience into a new similar situation can also be very helpful. If you found a way of coping with interview anxiety, you can reflect on what you did before to be in a more resourceful state for the next interview.

PERSONAL REALITY

As you can see in Figure 6, once you have filtered an experience through your deletions, distortions and generalizations, you create your map of that experience. This map is your interpretation of reality and, in NLP, is referred to as your "map of the world". You respond and react to your map of the world and not the experience itself!

Your response to your map of the world results in how you feel.

RESULTS

How you feel about something affects your general way of being (physically and emotionally) in any moment, also known as your state. Your state, made up of your thoughts, feelings and physiology, will have a big impact on your behaviour.

The process described above works from the inside out; that is your map of the world affecting your feelings, state and behaviour.

You can also influence your state from the outside in, by making changes to your physiology (see Chapter 17 *Presuppositions*).

Your state influences your behaviour, and your behaviour impacts your results.

MAPS
and my3lPractices

What if we could change some of our filters and, by doing this, change the meaning of an experience. How could that change the way we think, feel and act and therefore help us develop greater behavioural flexibility? How could that be part of a process that leads us to a life more aligned with our values?

The my31Practices approach helps you to actively influence your filters in a positive way by placing your values at the forefront of your awareness.

When we are more aware of how our own perceptions shape our map of the world, then we can also begin to be aware that if we can change those perceptions, we can change what we perceive as reality.

PAUSE FOR THOUGHT ...

How are your filters affecting what you are experiencing right now?

WANT TO KNOW MORE?

http://www.my31practices.com/the-book/resources/chapter-16

PRESUPPOSITIONS

"We cannot change the cards we are dealt, just how we play the hand."
Randy Pausch[i]

The NLP presuppositions[ii] are assumptions and beliefs that, though not necessarily true, have a positive impact on our achieving what we want when we act as if they are true.

As a human being, you have to give your experiences meaning. You make assumptions about events, other people and yourself all the time; for example; "it was great" or "it was awful", "I can do it!" or "I can't do it"; "he doesn't care" or "he does care". They are your beliefs and not necessarily fact.

The effect of presuppositions on your life is profound. They can hold you back or take you forward. If you expect something to be difficult, then it probably will be. If such assumptions are not actually true, if they are just things you tell yourself, how often do you presuppose things that have a negative impact on what you do?

Presuppositions are often revealed in your speech and behaviour. For example, if someone says, "I wish I was as good as you at networking", this presupposes two things; firstly that the speaker believes that you are good at networking and secondly, that they are not as good as you. The person saying this might find this presupposition demotivating, or, on the other hand, the presupposition may launch them into action. The key question is: What does the presupposition do for you?

The NLP presuppositions are assumptions and beliefs, or guiding principles, which if accepted as true, have a positive impact on your chances of success and fulfilment.[ii] Try out some of the presuppositions below by thinking about situations you have experienced in the past where you might not have achieved the outcome you wanted. Which of the presuppositions below could have brought about a more successful outcome?

Let's explore some of the NLP presuppositions that are particularly useful in the context of my31Practices.

1. There is no failure, there is only feedback.

> *"Feedback is the breakfast of champions."*
> *Ken Blanchard[iii]*

This presupposition highlights that experience is gained when you don't get what you want – a learning that creates a platform for improvement. Learning from your experience, or sometimes the experience of others, helps to avoid potential pitfalls and enables faster progress. There is nothing to be gained from beating yourself up when something goes wrong, and everything to be gained from focusing on what you learned and integrating that knowledge to get a better outcome next time.

Feedback plays such a critical function in our lives; it helps us learn from our mistakes. When feedback is poorly given, it tends to be poorly received. If feedback is given without a common positive intention, it becomes criticism, not feedback. Criticism disguised as feedback is usually resisted and rejected, thus blocking the learning process. Feedback exists as a measure of how effective we have been and to highlight how we could be even more effective. This also refers to feedback you give yourself. What does your inner voice say to you when you make errors or try things that do not work?

Consider this, if you are giving feedback to yourself or others, how important is it to pay attention to the language you use? Phrases such as "I/you did a terrible job", or "I/you failed" can be demotivating and move you further away from your objective. If, on the other hand, you choose phrases such as, "I/you know that doesn't work, so what could I/you do differently next time?" this is more likely to help you stay focused on the goal and move you towards it.

Those who are hungry for feedback and act on it tend to progress the fastest. Progress would be impossible without feedback. Take a look around you now. Almost everything you see is the result of multiple feedback loops, whether it is a chair, table, carpet, pen, car, street light or newspaper. Whatever it is, think how many times the designer and manufacturer must have tried something that didn't work and then was able to discard or build on whatever that was to find something that did work. We cannot progress without experimentation and feedback. When we learn to accept and embrace trial and error, feedback and revision, we increase our chances of success (see the Edison story in Chapter 12 *Practice*).

2. Flexibility is key.

> *"If you always do what you always did,*
> *you will always get what you always got."*
> Anonymous[v]

Your goal is your intention, and therefore any path that takes you there is a good path – as long as it is legal, ethical and ecologically sound. Having more than one way to achieve something will provide options in case one path becomes blocked. A former flying instructor once remarked: "In an emergency, if you can't land on the runway, land in a field; if you can't land in a field, land on a beach. Any landing you walk away from is a good landing." Flexibility comes from seeing the bigger picture and changing strategies when what you are doing no longer works.

If what you do doesn't work, it might not be the wisest strategy to simply repeat it.

When things are not working, do something else. Flexibility is key.

3. The mind and body are a connected system.

> *"The sound body is the product of the sound mind."*
> George Bernard Shaw[vi]

Inside out

Have you ever seen someone who is feeling down or nervous or anxious? Now think about someone who was super-confident, or really excited? What differences do you notice in posture or gestures in each case? NLP refers to a person's posture and gestures and other physical cues as physiology. Physiology in this sense is a form of non-verbal communication and is also known as body language.

When our feelings affect our physiology, or an internal feeling has an external manifestation, the process is working from the inside out.

Outside in

Altering your physiology will alter the way you feel. Try it for yourself now, look down at the ground, and let your shoulders drop and frown. Notice how quickly the way you feel changes emotionally. Hold this position for 30 seconds. Now stand upright with your shoulders back. Hold your head high with your chin slightly raised and smile. How quickly do you notice changes to the way you feel now? There is a link between physiology and chemical changes in the body (see Chapter 16 *Maps*). Watch professional athletes prepare for big moments and see if you can spot this psychophysical link, the relationship between mind and body. A change in physiology will affect how you feel, your state and your performance. There is also a mind/body effect that shows in physiology when you experience internal conflict between what your head tells you, your heart feels and your gut needs (see Chapter 21 *mBIT*).

When our physiology affects our feelings, or an external physical shift produces an internal shift in feelings, we can say that the process is working from the outside in.

Examples of the mind-body link can also be found in the world of theatre. Constantin Stanislavski,[vii] the father of modern actor training, developed what he called the "method of physical actions". This involves actors accessing states and emotions by making changes to their physiology.[viii]

There is mounting scientific evidence to support the notion that your mind can have an impact on your physical wellbeing.[ix]

4. **Respect for other people's map of the world.**

> *"Always respect another's opinion*
> *and another's point of view."*
> Sri Sathya Sai Baba[x]

In Chapter 16 *Maps* we share how you process the world around you through your unique set of filters, and, because of this, often see things differently from other people. It may be our similarities with other people that bring us together but it is the awareness of our differences that actually helps us to grow. Imagine if you went around just confirming what you already know, you wouldn't learn anything new. Respecting other people's viewpoints helps you form stronger relationships and connections through greater resonance and rapport (described in Chapter 18 *Awareness*). Listening to others is also often the source of expanding your knowledge and even questioning some of your own assumptions. You do not have to agree with the others' views, however, if you do not give them the space to express themselves, you might never know what you could have learned.

When have you changed your opinion recently as a result of hearing someone else's perspective?

5. **Checking change for ecology.**

> *"Sometimes your greatest strength can emerge as a weakness if the context changes."*
> *Harsha Bhogle[xi]*

In NLP, ecology refers to the study of consequences.[xii] Before making a change it is important to ask what the consequences of that change could be to you, those close to you and the environment around you. It is also important to consider the context for any change. If you want to be more assertive in the office, you might not want to be more assertive at home.

Have you made a change recently that turned out to have negative consequences for you or those around you?

As my31Practices is all about making change, this simple presupposition is important, particularly in the context of assessing the impact of change (see Chapter 14 *Assessment*).

6. **If it is possible for someone else, it is possible for you.**

> *"If you believe in yourself anything is possible."*
> *Miley Cyrus[xiii]*

If someone similar to you can achieve something, then you can too; the only question is how. As long as there are no physical or neurological reasons why you cannot achieve something, what can you do to get the same or similar results? Is there a strategy of thought, belief, or actions that someone else has that could help you? What does this someone else do to achieve what they achieve? Can you unearth their patterns? Is it to do with something they do physically? Is it a belief or set of beliefs that they hold?

Have you ever wanted to achieve something that someone else has, then worked towards it, and achieved it yourself? Do you know someone else that has done this? What did they do?

Often it is only your limiting beliefs about yourself that hold you back.

7. **You are in charge of your mind and therefore your results.**

> *"Take charge of your thoughts.*
> *You can do what you will with them."*
> *Plato[xiv]*

When you believe something is possible, you open the door to change. If you do not like the way you are thinking, change it. This is often to do with where you place your focus and the meaning you are giving to something.

Have you ever been thinking about an issue from a particular perspective and then consciously decided to look at that issue from a different perspective and felt more empowered as a result? Perhaps you have been working towards a goal and when you encountered obstacles you found it difficult to keep going. Have you ever got back on track by reminding yourself why that goal was important to you in the first place?

This is an example of being in charge of your mind and affecting your own results.

8. **If someone doesn't understand what you said, you have not communicated it.**

> *"The single biggest problem in communication is the illusion that it has taken place."*
> *George Bernard Shaw[xv]*

If others do not get your message you have not transmitted it well enough. How do you know others have not got your message? You can usually pick up on the signals through the expressions and body language of others. You can also ask the person a question to test their understanding. It is important to communicate effectively and that means making sure that you have provided information in a way that another person can understand. This might not be the obvious way to you.

Have you ever been misunderstood when you have thought you communicated effectively? Could you have done more to be sure that the meaning you intended was what the other person understood?

9. **There are no resistant people, only inflexible communicators. Resistance is a sign of a lack of rapport.**

    "It is not our differences that divide us. It is our inability to recognize, accept, and celebrate those differences."
    Audre Lorde[xvi]

    Resistance is often due to a lack of understanding or connection. If you encounter resistance, notice what happens when you increase your understanding of the position of the other person. Resistance reduces as rapport increases. When it comes to working with others, or when looking to motivate, influence or inspire others, rapport is one of the most powerful tools you have available.

PRESUPPOSITIONS
- in practice

Try out some of the NLP presuppositions by thinking about situations you have experienced in the past where you have not got the outcome you wanted. Which of the presuppositions below, if you had adopted them at the time, could have brought about a more successful outcome?

As you try these presuppositions for yourself, reflect on the process of "identify", "action", "impact" and "refine" (see Chapter 3 *How*).

PRESUPPOSITIONS
and my31Practices

As you seek greater alignment with your personal values by using my31Practices, the presuppositions can help you stay focused and sometimes push through when a task seems challenging. Whenever you find something in your daily tasks a challenge, see what happens when you apply some of these filters.

How do these presuppositions apply to my31Practices?

1. There is no failure, only feedback: It might be that some of your myPractices will be rejected or made more difficult by people you come into contact with. In this case, take whatever learnings you can that enable you to progress positively forward.

2. Flexibility is Key: As the "how" you implement your myPractice is so important, be prepared to be flexible to be able to carry it out. If you have decided to call a friend and then you see them in a café, why not go and say hello?

3. The mind and body are a connected system: Be aware of how your feelings are affecting you and your approach to your day. If you feel it would be a good idea to change your state to a more positive one, change your physiology.

4. Respect other people's maps of the world: Listen to others. If you sense that someone may not respond to you for one reason or another, change the way you respond to them to create or maintain a good relationship.

5. Evaluate what change you want to make, where and what the consequences would be: Consider where and when you are planning to implement your my31Practices and make sure you have thought about the impact your behaviour would have on others.

6. If it is possible in the world, it's possible for you: Keep motivated by reminding yourself that you can do this.

7. You are in charge of your mind and therefore your results: Stay positive and forward thinking. If you start to doubt yourself, do something about it.

8. If someone doesn't understand what you have said, you have not communicated it: Be clear at all times. Understand your myPractices well and when you are engaging with other people as part of your myPractices, make sure you are communicating in a way they can understand – and check for understanding by asking questions.

9. There are no resistant people, only inflexible communicators. Resistance is a sign of a lack of rapport: Always build and maintain rapport when implementing your myPractices.

PAUSE FOR THOUGHT ...

Which presuppositions from the list above will you use to help your implementation of my31Practices?

WANT TO KNOW MORE?

http://www.my31practices.com/the-book/resources/chapter-17

AWARENESS

"Every human has four endowments – self-awareness, conscience, independent will and creative imagination. These give us the ultimate human freedom ... The power to choose, to respond, to change."
Stephen R. Covey[i]

Awareness plays a central role in Chapter 7 *Mindfulness*. In NLP, awareness is what you perceive and goes hand in hand with calibration, which is described by NLP co-creator John Grinder, as noticing change.

Figure 7. The awareness, calibration and feedback loop[ii]

You cannot calibrate change without first being aware of "what" is changing. Awareness can be static, whereas calibration has a more dynamic element to it. Figure 7, The awareness, calibration and feedback loop (page 193) shows that without awareness and calibration, feedback is not possible.

For example, if you meet someone and his or her expression is neutral, you may "sense" or be aware of this neutrality. If this person then asks you who you are and you explain that you know a good friend of theirs, they might then become more open and perhaps start to smile. You are likely to notice this change in their physiology and expression from neutrality to smile. In NLP, this dynamic awareness is referred to as calibration. In this example, as you realize the person is more engaged with you, you might begin to feel more relaxed. This relaxation is the result of the feedback you have given yourself based on what you have noticed about the situation and how it changed.

> *"Awareness is the greatest agent for change."*
> *Eckhart Tolle[iii]*

Grinder describes calibration as the "mother of all skill sets" because if you cannot notice the changes in and around you, you cannot respond to those changes. The ability to be flexible and change in response to changes in your environment is one of the pillars of NLP and a key component to the "principles of success". Imagine what would happen if you were talking to someone and you did not pick up on the signals they were sending you; for example, that they were bored, or that they wanted to say something, or that they were indicating that they were pressed for time.

How would your ability to be more aware and calibrate help you in this kind of situation?

Similarly, if you are unaware that you are running an unhelpful pattern of behaviour, how are you going to be able to change it? Awareness opens the door to feedback and change.

Robert Dilts developed the B.A.G.E.L Model[iv] as "a simple means to identify the key behavioural cues used by NLP to summarize the internal processes of others."[v]. This model can help you communicate more effectively by raising awareness of internal shifts or processing in others by noticing their external cues. Noticing these shifts enables you to adapt your behaviour in order to communicate more effectively.

FEEDBACK LOOPS

In your day-to-day life you are experiencing feedback loops all the time and these give you a clue as to what to do next. When you talk to other people, you are usually scanning for signs of connection, understanding, resonance and so on. When you watch two people speaking, pay attention to how the listener will often nod their head or make sounds such as "uh huh". This is valuable feedback for the speaker.

To demonstrate our need for feedback, find someone to talk to and when they are speaking, keep your head perfectly still, do not make any gestures or sounds, keep your face completely expressionless and just look at them neutrally. Notice how this absence of feedback quickly causes the other person to become uncomfortable because they have nothing to respond to.

The next time you meet someone, be aware of the tone in their voice, their gestures, their energy shifts. What is this non-verbal communication telling you about how they feel and how do you respond to it?

If you have already created your list of myPractices, you might have found that some were easy to define and that there were others which you were less certain of. How did that lack of certainty show itself in your physiology and/or tonality? Did you notice what your eyes were doing as you searched for what your myPractices could be?

It is obvious that you can be aware of things that are tangible, such as objects, other people, the weather and so on. But you can also be aware of things that are less tangible, such as how you feel about something, including when something "just doesn't feel right".

This is very true when it comes to your values. Although you can be consciously aware of some of your values, often they are out of your conscious awareness, sitting in your subconscious. You become more aware of these values when they are being honoured or compromised.

By way of example, have you experienced a situation where everything just seemed "right", where relationships, actions, decisions, results were all so easy, enjoyable and successful? It is likely that your values were being honoured.

On the other side of the coin, have you ever been asked to do something and you had a funny feeling about it? It just didn't feel right? Did you sense some form of discomfort internally, perhaps in your gut? This was likely to be a subconscious signal telling you that one of your values was being compromised – see the activity in Chapter 6 *Values*.

INTENTION AND AWARENESS

As mentioned in Chapter 16 *Maps*, the cognitive psychologist, George A Miller, proposed that we can only be aware of between five and nine bits of information at any moment of time, known more widely as the "seven, plus or minus two". If we overload the "seven, plus or minus two", if we add more information to what we are consciously processing, something has to drop out.[vi]

Take the example of a waiter or waitress in a restaurant. They might have a long list of specials for the day. As they begin to go through their list, which they have repeated numerous times earlier that day, notice what happens if you suddenly interrupt them with an unrelated question, such as commenting on what they are wearing. Usually this throws them so that they forget what they were saying or where they were in their list because you have put a whole new set of thoughts into their conscious awareness. What about you? Has anyone ever distracted you by asking a question unrelated to what you were doing and then suddenly you forgot what you were doing? This is a product of our conscious mind's limited ability to process multiple tasks.

As the conscious mind is limited in its capacity to process information, there are some things that we simply cannot be aware of in any one moment. When we set an intention, we tend to focus on what is connected to that intention, and we are not aware of other things. This certainly helps us focus, but at the same time produces blind spots.

Gestalt therapy founder, Fritz Perls, uses the setting of a cocktail party to highlight how intention directs our awareness. If a designer walked into a cocktail party, it is likely that he or she would notice the décor, clothes, colours and so on. Certain things would be in the foreground and others would fade into the background, or not be noticed at all. What would an electrician be more likely to notice and what would they miss?

> *"Our intention creates our reality."*
> *Wayne W Dyer[vii]*

Your intention directs your attention, which directs your awareness and you respond to what you are aware of.[viii] What this means is that when you focus your attention somewhere, you may become unaware of other things.

In terms of relationships, being aware of non-verbal communication such as physiology, tone and calibrating shifts and changes can make a huge difference.

CALIBRATION
- in practice

Have a conversation with someone. Ask the other person to talk about something or someone they like. Notice the following:

Physiology: Their gestures, colour flushes, pupil dilation, breathing, energy shifts.

Tonality: Tone of voice, pitch, tempo, rhythm, timbre.

Words: Choice of words, which words they place special emphasis on.

Next, get them to shake off whatever state they are in to get into a neutral state. Then ask them to talk about something or someone they do not like. Notice the same things: physiology, tonality, words.

How do the two responses differ? Can you spot differences in physiology, tonality and words? How important is the physiology, tonality and words to the overall "feel" in each case?

According to psychologists Albert Mehrabian and Susan Ferris, where like and dislike is concerned, the meaning in a person's communication is transmitted 55% in their physiology, 38% in the person's tonality, and only 7% by the words.[ix]

Here's another example: If you asked someone if they enjoyed your performance in a play, or a meal you had cooked and they:

Physiology: glanced away.

Tonality: hesitated and sounded unsure.

Words: Used the words, "Yes, I thought it was really great".

How would you feel?

You are more likely to believe the messages being transmitted in the non-verbal cues, than the words "yes, I thought it was great", because you have noticed how the person was before the question was asked and calibrated the changes that followed the question.

Awareness and calibration skills are like muscles, the more attention you give them the more developed they become.

PERCEPTION

Perception is all about awareness. You can only respond to what you are aware of. Anthropologist Gregory Bateson, said that to really understand any situation fully, you need to examine it from at least three different perspectives. Take the example of a disagreement between you and someone else. There will be your opinion, the other person's opinion, and then what a neutral observer may see.

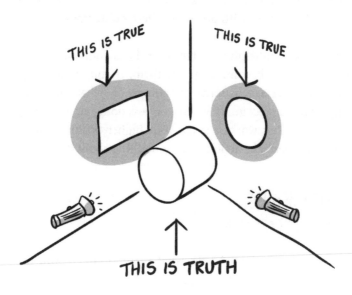

Figure 8. Truth perspective

Take a look at Figure 8, Truth perspective (page 201). From one perspective a person might be certain that they are looking at a circle, from a different perspective another person might be convinced that the object is a rectangle, and yet from another perspective, the truth becomes more apparent.

How often do you view something from just one perspective? What more might you discover when you take a different viewpoint?

Being aware that a situation's meaning could change depending on how you look at it enables us to make more informed choices, with potentially better outcomes.

To change unhelpful patterns of behaviour or habits you must first become aware of them. If you are looking to change certain patterns of thought or behaviour, it is important to recognize when you are doing or thinking something that works against your higher positive intention, and then take action to do something about it.

AWARENESS
and my31Practices

When you are aligned with what is important to you (ie your values), your physiology, tonality and words are all saying the same thing. You walk the talk. You are congruent. When your physiology, tone and words are giving mixed messages, it could be that there is something that is not aligned. By having a strong sense of awareness you can confirm when alignment is in place and take action when it is not.

The my31Practices approach supports this awareness through the framework of identification, action, impact and refinement (see Chapter 3 *How*).

PAUSE FOR THOUGHT ...

What are you noticing and being aware of at this moment that you were not aware of before?

WANT TO KNOW MORE?

http://www.my31practices.com/the-book/resources/chapter-18

ALIGNMENT

TRANSFORMATIONAL

- MISSION / PURPOSE
- IDENTITY
- VALUES & BELIEFS

BEYOND SELF

TRANSACTIONAL

- CAPABILITIES & SKILLS
- BEHAVIOUR
- ENVIRONMENT

"Just as your car runs more smoothly and requires less energy to go faster when the wheels are in alignment, you perform better when your thoughts, feelings, emotions, goals and values are in balance."
Brian Tracy[i]

In neuro-linguistic programming (NLP), alignment is the process of ensuring that all the elements involved in the successful completion of a desired outcome are optimized and in harmony to provide the greatest chance of success. In other words, the thoughts, feelings, words and actions are all saying the same thing. This is known as congruence or inner and outer equilibrium.

In relation to goals, NLP is concerned with alignment between:

1. Actions and goals (do your actions help you achieve your goals?)

2. Actions and values (are your actions congruent with what is important to you?)

3. Goals and the environment from an ecological perspective (what can you do to make sure that the goal does not harm you, other people or the environment?)[ii]

There are a number of alignment processes in the NLP toolkit. One of the most powerful is Robert Dilts' Neuro-Logical Levels of Change. The model explores six levels of human experience. When you explore these levels in relation to a goal, for example, you can identify how aligned your goal is, and put strategies in place to align any elements that are not aligned. The model is also very useful for exploring the various roles you play in your life, such as parent, friend, provider, colleague and others.

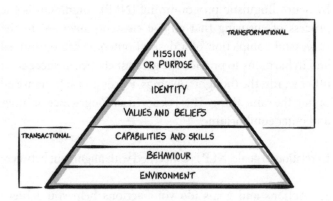

Figure 9. Neuro-Logical Levels of Change: reproduced with kind permission from Robert Dilts

In Figure 9 above, you will notice that the bottom three levels feel more transactional. This means that they are tangible; where you are, what you do, and what abilities you have. Changes made in these areas are more likely to be carried out consciously. The top three levels are more transformational; values, beliefs, sense of identity and purpose. They operate at a more subconscious level. These higher levels have a great impact on the lower levels, for example, your values drive your behaviour. If being compassionate to others is important to you (value), then you may find yourself automatically giving up your seat on a bus (behaviour) to someone who you believe needs it more than you.

NEURO-LOGICAL LEVELS
and my3lPractices

> *"Your alignment trumps everything."*
> *Abraham Hicks*

To explore the model, why not use one of your own myPractices goals? We'll take the hypothetical example of the myValue "compassion" and the associated myPractice "I proactively offer help to other people".

When using the model, it is often more powerful to write out each level on separate pieces of paper, as in Figure 10 on the next page. Place each piece of paper on the floor as the diagram shows, starting with "environment" and finishing with "mission" or "purpose". Step through each level in turn and, as you do so, explore each level through a series of questions. Once you have reached "mission" or "purpose" turn around and come back down the levels to "environment", before stepping into a neutral reflective observer position.

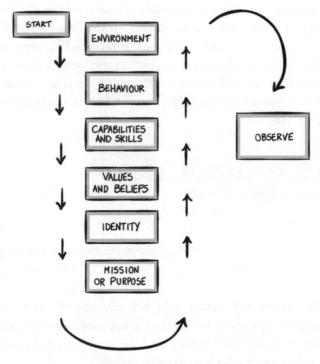

Figure 10. The Neuro-Logical Levels of Change Process

NEURO-LOGICAL LEVELS OF CHANGE
- in practice

To get the most from this process, it is important to reflect on and consider each question as fully as you can.

The idea of each level is to recognize any misalignment and explore how you could bring that level into alignment.

Step 1: ENVIRONMENT: Physical locations and people.
Questions:

Who in your environment affects your ability to proactively offer help to other people?

Who in your environment hinders you or holds you back from proactively offering help to other people (this can be in the form of people telling you that you can't do it, you're not that type of person, etc.)? If there is anyone who does this, what can you do about it so that it does not create a block for you?

When do you proactively offer help to other people? Where do you proactively offer help to other people? Where do you not proactively offer help to other people? Where might it be appropriate for you not to proactively offer help to other people?

What could you change in your environment that would make it more conducive to you proactively offering help to other people in the way you would like?

When you have explored this level fully, you can progress to the next step.

Step 2: BEHAVIOUR: What you do.
Questions:

What do you currently do that helps you to proactively offer help to other people?

What do you currently do that gets in the way of you proactively offering help to other people?

What behaviours could you display that would enable you to proactively offer help to other people more often?

(Note: This step can help you define your my31Practices practices/actions)

When you have explored this fully, you can progress to the next step.

Step 3: CAPABILITIES AND SKILLS: What you are able to do or capable of doing.

Questions:

What capabilities or skills do you have that help you to proactively offer help to other people?

How could you up-skill or develop in a way that would help you to proactively offer help to other people?

When you have explored this fully, you can progress to the next step.

Step 4: VALUES AND BELIEFS: Why living this value is important to you.

Questions:

Why is proactively offering help to other people important to you?

Are there any beliefs that act as potential barriers to you proactively offering help to other people?

What beliefs do you have that help you to proactively offer help to other people in the way that you want to?

When you have explored this fully, you can progress to the next step.

Step 5: IDENTITY: Your sense of self.

Questions:

How does proactively offering help to other

people fit with your sense of who you truly are?
Imagine proactively offering help to other people in the way you want to and notice if that "feels right". If there is anything that you do not feel sure about, what could the reason be?

When you have explored this fully, you can progress to the next step.

Step 6: MISSION OR PURPOSE: What is this really about, beyond you?

What impact does your behaviour of proactively offering help to other people have beyond you?

How does your behaviour of proactively offering help to other people benefit other people and how could they in turn then benefit others they come in to contact with?

What "ripple effect" does your behaviour of proactively offering help to other people have that emanates beyond you?

If you were to think of an example or metaphor that would represent this sense of mission or purpose, what might it be?

Note: Metaphors can be powerful because they encapsulate far more about an experience than a simple description can (see Chapter 8 *Metaphor*). Now you have reached the sixth level, turn around and begin the journey back to ENVIRONMENT, again exploring each level as you go. Focus your attention on how different the return journey feels at each level.

Step onto IDENTITY.

Step 7: IDENTITY
Questions:
Bringing your sense of your mission or purpose with you, how does proactively offering help to other people fit with your sense of your identity now?
When you have connected with this, you can progress to the next step.

Step 8: VALUES AND BELIEFS
Questions:
Bringing your sense of mission or purpose and your identity with you, why is proactively offering help to other people important to you now?
What are your beliefs now?
When you have explored this fully, you can progress to the next step.

Step 9: CAPABILITIES AND SKILLS
Questions:
Bringing your mission or purpose, your identity and your values and beliefs with you, what capabilities do you have to help you proactively offer help to other people? Is there anything you could do to up-skill now?
When you have explored this fully, you can progress to the next step.

Step 10: BEHAVIOUR

Questions:

Bringing your mission or purpose, your identity, your values and beliefs and your capabilities and skills with you, what do you do that is in alignment with proactively offering help to other people?

What do you currently do to proactively offer help to other people?

What could you do now that would help you express proactively offering help to other people even more?

(This step can help you define your my31Practices affirmations (see Chapter 9 *Affirmation*).

When you have explored this fully, you can progress to the next step.

Step 11: ENVIRONMENT

What changes could you make to your environment now?

Having explored each level on the way up and down, move to a neutral position and reflect on the journey and whatever you have learned at each level, and how that can help you express your value more fully.

This model can be extremely powerful in helping you to explore a goal or role (see Chapter 22 *Goals*).

OCCUPATIONAL STRESS[iii]

Have you ever calculated what proportion of your waking hours you spend at work? For most people, it is a significant fraction. You don't need us to tell you that your working day is a huge influence on your life, your values and your personal alignment. Just imagine if you have a job environment in which you are regularly experiencing conflict with your values. This can lead to stress-related symptoms and, in the worst case, stress-related illness. You will see in Chapter 2 *Why* that in the UK alone, there are nearly ten million working days lost in a year through illness.[iv]

Of course, there is much that managers and leaders in the workplace can do to reduce these statistics.[v] The topic of organizational values alignment is the focus of the first 31Practices book and it is an approach that benefits everybody. Research shows that those individuals who are clear about their personal values are not only happier and more fulfilled, but are also up to 17% more engaged at work than people who do not have that clarity.[vi] Interestingly, they found that when the organization's values are all that employees know about, there is a slight negative impact, taking commitment 0.5% below the norm. Imagine the positive impact in workplaces if recruitment and selection, performance review and employee engagement initiatives were aligned with employees' personal values.

While organizations can play an important role, ultimately, alignment with your values is your personal responsibility. The job you do and your workplace environment have a major bearing on your values and behaviour alignment, so taking a values perspective is important. This may not always be easy and sometimes the choices may be limited. All we are suggesting is that it is worth the time and effort to make a conscious choice.

ALIGNMENT
and my31Practices

In summary, to align with your values, you first need to be aware of what your values are. This is the first step of the my31Practices process. Having identified your values, you then decide on a set of myPractices that express your chosen values, in a very practical, tangible way. You can use the features on www.my31Practices.com to motivate you and provide the support to live in line with these values and practices on a daily basis. This leads to a greater sense of self-fulfillment and congruence – or authentic happiness.

PAUSE FOR THOUGHT ...

How can the Neuro-Logical Levels of Change process help you to develop and practice your set of 31 myPractices?

WANT TO KNOW MORE?

http://www.my31practices.com/the-book/resources/chapter-19

BELIEFS

BELIEFS ≠ FACTS

"It's not the events of our lives that shape us,
but our beliefs as to what those events mean."
Tony Robbins[i]

Empowering beliefs can have a positive impact on your life and the goals you set (see Chapter 9 *Affirmation*). In this chapter, we focus on limiting beliefs, as they can provide the biggest hurdle for you to overcome along the journey to your goals.

Beliefs are not facts – otherwise we would call them facts. They are your best guesses about the world around you, about yourself and others.

Fact	(Limiting) Belief
I did not pass my exam	I cannot pass exams

Beliefs are the glue that holds our model of reality together.[ii] They are generalizations about experience. It could be that you recognize loose beliefs as opinions, and beliefs with multiple references as being true. However, beliefs are still not facts. It is important to be aware of the difference between a belief and a fact.

Facts are irrefutable – e.g. night follows day is a fact of life on Earth.

Beliefs are judgments/interpretations or assumptions – e.g. you shouldn't listen to other people.

Just like values, beliefs are largely context specific. What is important to you in a relationship might not be what is important to you in a work context. You might believe it is right to be assertive at work, but that you need to be sensitive in a family relationship, for example. We may have values and beliefs that cross all contexts, these are our core values (the arena of my31Practices) and beliefs, such as the value of honesty and belief that "stealing is wrong".

BELIEFS ABOUT VALUES

"If I do not believe as you believe, it proves that you do not believe as I believe, and that is all that it proves."
Thomas Paine[iii]

In neuro-linguistic programming (NLP), establishing your values and placing them in a hierarchy can be extremely useful in helping you understand your behaviours. Values are crucial to help you stay motivated, build relationships, resolve conflicts, make decisions, and set goals.

Your values and beliefs combine to form your attitudes.

A MEANS TO AN END?

It is important to understand the difference between "means" values and "ends" values.

Means values: These are values that are our steps towards an ends value, e.g. money may be a means value that supports the ends value of freedom.

Ends values: These are fully grounded values and do not lead to a further value – perhaps "family" for example. You can test this by asking a follow-up question when "family" is stated as a value: "And why is that important to you?" If there is no answer, this possibly indicates that the value is grounded.

VALUES IDENTIFICATION

To identify your values, try asking yourself these questions: What is most important to me personally in life?

What do I value most in my life?

What do I want for my life?

For each value you come up with, ask the follow up question that is designed to identify the ends value that may lie beneath the value given. The follow-up question is: "And why is that important to me?" Ask this question three times to get to the ends value, e.g.

1. Q. What do I want for my life?
          A. Wealth.

2. Q. Why is wealth important to me?
          A. Because it brings me choice.

3. Q. Why is choice important to me?
          A. Because it brings me a sense of freedom.

In this case "freedom" is the ends value and wealth and choice are means values. Now you know that the ends value is freedom, you can find many different ways to satisfy this value in terms of the behaviours you could adopt.

ENDS VALUES: SO WHAT

Let's continue with the example where you say one of your values is wealth. If you do not go further to understand why wealth is important to you, you might just focus on making money and lose sight of what the value is actually intended to support. Exploring this example further, you might say that wealth is important because it brings choice and ultimately the ends value of a sense of freedom. Once you know what the ends value is, you have the option of finding other ways to satisfy the value, not just through wealth. It could be that chasing money could actually lead to spending less time making choices which would work against your true ends value of a sense of freedom, and cause internal conflict between your values and your behaviour. It could be for instance, that self employment rather than a higher paid corporate role would be more aligned with an ends value of sense of freedom.

VALUES HIERARCHY

In NLP, it is often useful to establish a values hierarchy – a list of values sorted into levels of importance. This can be useful in the context of work for example, where certain jobs satisfy certain values but not all. When you know your values hierarchy in the context of work, you can see which job satisfies the most important values.

To create a values hierarchy, you can make a list of your top ten values. Then arrange them in the order of importance to you. Please note: by placing your values in an order you are not dismissing any of them.

Having placed your values in an order, take the top five and place them in a group labelled B. Now take the bottom five values and place them in a group labelled A.

Examine the groups. If you could choose only one group, which group would it be? It is important to make sure that you go with your "gut" instinct. The moment you begin to rationalize your decision with your conscious mind, the results become clouded by logic rather than what you unconsciously "feel" is right for you. If you have chosen group A, then your values are probably not in the right hierarchy.

If you did choose group A, and you wanted to know exactly what your hierarchy is, you could take the top two values and ask yourself: "If I could have only one of these, which would I choose, value 1 or 2?" If you choose value 2, swap the top two values on your list. If you choose value

1, then add value 3 and ask: "If I could have only one of these, which would I choose, value 1 or 3?" Continue to work through the list until you have judged all the values in this way.

You can also consider combining values. For example, if you have the values "excellence" and "success" in your final ten. What do these words mean to you? You may conclude that your value is "excellence" with the definition "delivering the best for success".

As a final "sense check", look at your top five values and consider them as a set, rather than five individual values in isolation. When you consider the definitions of this set of values, does this describe you, your essence?

VALUES AND BELIEFS

What a value means to you is the product of beliefs you hold about that value. Take a value such as "respect". The word "respect" is a label. As such, it might mean one thing to you and quite another thing to someone else. Your belief might be that holding the door open for others is a mark of respect, while somebody else might not share that view. It is important to define what you believe the value means to you (see Chapter 3 *How*).

Consider the example below. The table reflects what a guest and their host believes "respect" to mean, and how they interpret it.

Value: Respect	
Guest	**Host**
Belief (respect = …)	**Belief** (respect = …)
Making breakfast for me.	Helping my guest feel at home by letting them do their own thing. They know where the kitchen is, they can help themselves to whatever they want for breakfast. They don't want me fussing over them. That would be disrespectful.
Taking time off work to be with me while I am visiting.	Leaving my guest to relax while I am at work.
Providing a timetable of activities.	Not overloading my guest with things to do; seeing how the moment takes them.

There is a significant difference between what the host and guest believe about what the value "respect" means and, in this case, it could lead to misunderstandings. You might share the same value "label" with somebody else, but what you believe the label to mean can be different to, or even polar opposites from, the other person. What is important is to have a clear understanding of what the "label" means to you and to others.

The meanings you assign to your values are effectively your value judgments. Value judgments are simply beliefs.

Beliefs are not fixed; they can change over time.

We have the ability to change the way we think, to lay down new patterns of thinking and make old patterns of thinking fade to distant memories. This process is known in neuroscience as neuroplasticity.[iv]

> "The statement that 'the mind is only what the brain does' is a statement that only makes sense in a pre-neuroplastic era. Now that we know that mind also changes brain, should we not equally say that 'the brain is what mind does?'"
> Norman Doidge[v]

Neuroplasticity has tremendous health implications; it also offers evidence that "positive thinking" really can make a positive impact on our lives.[vi]

How many beliefs have you changed since you were a child? At one point, you might have believed that ghosts existed. Do you still believe that today?

Take a few moments to think back to when you were 15 years old. What was important to you then? What did you believe then?

Now jump forward to when you were 21 years old. What was important to you at 21? What did you believe at 21?

There might be some things that were the same, how many things were different? For example, perhaps at the age of 15 you were not working. At 21 you might have had a job and new responsibilities, especially if you had also started a family. What was important to you and what you believed might have shifted considerably. To what extent has what was important to you and what you believed shifted?

Our beliefs can change due to life events, influences from friends, work, environment and many other factors.

"The greatest discovery of my generation is that human beings can alter their lives by altering their attitudes of mind."
William James[vii]

BELIEF CHANGE

"If you don't change your beliefs, your life will be like this forever. Is that good news?"
W Somerset Maugham[viii]

Beliefs that do not serve you limit you. Limiting beliefs are one of the main barriers to successfully achieving goals.

One method to start the process of overcoming a limiting belief is to cast doubt over the belief itself. This opens the door to a possible new more empowering belief.

If you can cast doubt over a limiting belief, then that automatically opens up space for new possibilities. You cannot possibly have doubt without creating space for new possibilities, and new possibilities can lead to a new outcome.

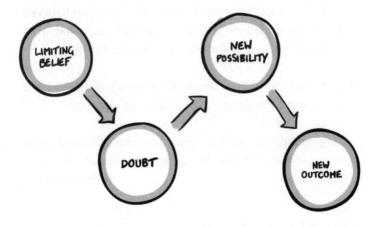

Figure 11. Loosening limiting beliefs

Look at the example below from a conversation between two people:

Person A: My friend was late; they obviously don't care about me, (this is the limiting belief).
Person B: How do you know that?
Person A: Because they were late.
Person B: So, being late means you don't care?
Person A: Yes.
Person B: Have you ever been late to meet someone and yet you did care about him or her?
Person A: (pause) Yes, I suppose so.

This interaction has Person A casting doubt over his or her own limiting belief. Asking questions like this is always going to be more powerful in terms of belief change, in that you are indirectly telling someone that their belief is wrong. It is Person A who casts doubt on his or her own belief.

> *"Beliefs are many but truth is one."*
> *Debasish Mridha[ix]*

Although the above scenario involves two people, there is no reason why you could not carry out this process on your own with your own beliefs, especially if you recognize that a particular belief is causing you to feel bad or holding you back.

LANGUAGE AND LIMITING BELIEFS

> *"But if thought corrupts language,*
> *language can also corrupt thought."*
> *George Orwell, 1984[x]*

Limiting beliefs are often revealed through the words people use. The NLP Meta Model[xi] is a language model that looks at how your words reveal some of your internal filters, including limiting beliefs.

Necessity, possibility and impossibility are categories of Model Operators within the Meta Model. They can reveal limiting beliefs. The table below shows some of these patterns and questions to cast doubt on the limiting belief.

RESISTING CHANGE

When you are maintaining a limiting belief and effectively resisting change, do you ever find yourself using one of the following strategies: look for things that confirm the limiting belief, refuse to consider anything that may contradict the belief, put a "spin" on anything that challenges the limiting belief by calling it an exception?

Modal Operators and their Meta Model Challenges[xii]		
Necessity	**Possibility**	**Impossibility**
Have to, need to, must, should (challenge the previous four patterns by asking: Says who? What would happen if you didn't?), must not, should not (challenge the previous two patterns by asking: Says who? What would happen if you did?)	Could, can, will, possible	Couldn't, can't, won't (challenge the previous three patterns by asking: What prevents you? What would happen if you did?), impossible (challenge this pattern by asking: What makes it impossible? What would happen if it wasn't?)

OVERCOMING LIMITING BELIEFS

In contrast, have you ever challenged one of your limiting beliefs by simply being open to exploring other more positive meanings, looking for evidence that contradicts the belief or actively seek new viewpoints to find positive interpretations or beliefs?

IDENTIFYING LIMITING BELIEFS

Limiting beliefs usually reveal themselves through language, physiology and behaviour. Limiting beliefs may be expressed as feelings such as, "I feel that this would be a disaster", or comparisons such as "I'm not as good as them". Often language patterns can reveal limiting beliefs, phrases that include words such as "have to", "need to", "should", "must", and so on.

NLP BELIEF CHANGE[xiii]

Below are some ways to change beliefs, many of them conversational. NLP uses a mixture of two language patterns when working with beliefs, the Meta Model for specificity and the Milton Model[xiv] to be artfully vague. The Milton Model was developed from the linguistic patterns of renowned hypnotherapist Milton H Erickson[xv] and is a set of patterns used to influence and erase resistance to ideas.

Look for examples that disprove the rule: Ask when or where this has not been true, e.g. "Nobody likes me", question: "Nobody? I like you". The belief is now no longer true.

Look at it from another angle: When you see things from another perspective you can change the way you view a situation. "I got 78% in my exam, that's rubbish", "I got 62% in my exam, I would be so happy with 78%!".

Reframe: "Dinner wasn't very tasty", "At least you had dinner, I missed it, and now I'm starving!".

Check the reality: how do you know? "I'm late, there's no point in going now", "How do you know that? What could happen if you did go?"

Upskill: "I can't train people to do the job, I don't know enough about it", "If you studied and gained experience, could you train people then?"

Act as if ...: Fake it until you make it. If you act confident, those around you will treat you as if you are confident, and that in turn will make you genuinely more confident.

Model yourself: Remember a time when you could do something, and then repeat what you did back then in the present situation.

Values: Remind yourself why something is important to you! "I can't do this!", "Why did you want to do this in the first place? Why is it important to you? What will you be able to do once you achieve this?"

You've changed beliefs before: "I can't do this", "Have you said that about something else in the past and then gone on to do it? Couldn't this be another one of those times?"

BELIEFS
and my31Practices

Beliefs support values. Your myPractices within my31Practices reflect your beliefs about behaviours that support your values, e.g. my value is "gratitude" and I believe that saying "thank you" when I receive something is the right thing to do for me to express this value.

As we mentioned in Chapter 6 *Values*, values often exist under the radar of awareness. You may discover you have a value when it is brought into focus. This could be because the value is being compromised and you feel bad. On the other hand, it could be because your value is being honoured and you feel great. Having raised awareness of a value in this way, you can now explore your beliefs around that value. This understanding is necessary to enable you to design strategies and behaviours that help you live a more authentic life. These strategies involve beliefs about what your values mean to you.

As well as being aware of empowering beliefs in connection with your values and my31Practices, it is useful to be aware of limiting beliefs so you can do something about them. One of the quickest ways of unveiling your limiting beliefs is asking yourself why you have not already achieved the goals you set for yourself. This might be helpful if, for some reason, you are not practicing one of your myPractices as well as you would like.

PAUSE FOR THOUGHT ...

What limiting beliefs do you hold, and what are you going to do about them?

WANT TO KNOW MORE?

http://www.my31practices.com/the-book/resources/chapter-20

MBIT

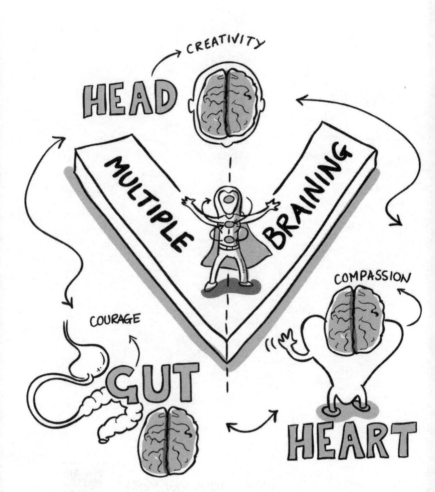

"You have to master not only the art of listening to your head, you must also master listening to your heart and listening to your gut."
Carly Fiorina[i]

Science tells us that we have at least three brains. For some people reading this, the idea of us having three brains may be challenging thinking. You may prefer to think of these "brains" as three clusters of complex neural networks or intelligences that form connections, retain memory and influence our decisions. The head brain, or cephalic brain, is the one that most people are aware of.

Think about this for a minute, where do some of your strongest decisions come from? There are times when your head leads your decision-making. What about at other times? Have you ever heard anybody say "I went with my heart" or "It was gut instinct"?

Before you read on, see Figure 12, The three brains on page 236 and have a go at drawing your version of the other two brains in the empty boxes.

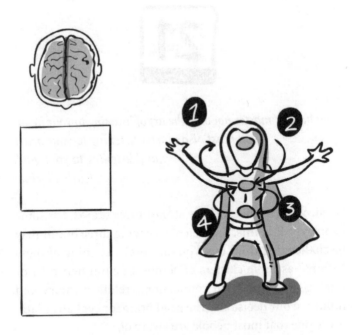

Figure 12. The three brains

Multiple Brain Integration Techniques (mBIT)

mBIT is a product of combining neuro-linguistic programming (NLP), neuroscience and positive psychology and was developed in Australia in around 2012 by international leadership consultant Grant Soosalu, and world leading behavioural modelling specialist and NLP Master Trainer Marvin Oka. Grant and Marvin have uncovered a large body of scientific evidence that underpins the foundations and presuppositions of mBIT. They have also formalized this into a process for aligning our three brains (head, or cephalic; heart, or cardiac; and gut, or enteric) to bring about ecological goal-related outcomes.

mBIT and mBraining[ii] is a new and exciting field, so let's begin with a couple of useful definitions:

mBraining: mBraining, or "multiple braining", is the way you are using your multiple brains and the process of aligning and integrating them for specific outcomes.[iii]

mBIT: Multiple Brain Integration Techniques is a suite of practical techniques for communicating with, aligning and harnessing the intelligence of your multiple brains.

THE SCIENCE BIT

> *"There are receptors to these molecules in your immune system, in your gut and in your heart. So when you say, "I have a gut feeling" or "my heart is sad", or "I am bursting with joy", you are not speaking metaphorically. You're speaking literally."*
> *Deepak Chopra[iv]*

What do we mean by "brains"?

Brains are complex neural networks with certain characteristics:[v]

- Sensory neurons and motor neurons – the head brain has more than 86 billion neurons, the heart has 30,000–120,000 neurons, and the gut has 500 million neurons.
- Neurons connecting in complex ways with other neurons.

- Support cells and components such as glial cells, astrocytes, proteins, etc.
- Functional attributes: perceiving and assimilating information, processing information, memory storage and access, the ability to learn.
- Can function independently of the head brain.
- A chemical warehouse of neurotransmitters.

While advances in science enable us to measure things we couldn't before, it is also interesting to see how more and more evidence is being uncovered to prove what ancient wisdoms have been saying for millennia, e.g. that the mind and body are facets of one holistic system. There are many research papers exploring the effect of meditation and mindfulness on stress relief and high blood pressure.[vi]

mBIT brings an interesting perspective and set of tools for working with personal alignment, utilizing the three main intelligences. It has a solid neuro-scientific base and is supported by the core skills of NLP and positive psychology.[vii] Also, see Chapter 19 *Alignment*.

BUILDING AWARENESS

At certain times you may sense that mainly it is your head influencing your decision-making: logical thoughts, practical and pragmatic, having to make sense of things and control events.

At other times you may sense that primarily it is your heart[viii] influencing your decision-making: things you love, your emotions, empathy or sympathy, compassion, a sense of good and bad, and right or wrong.

Sometimes you may sense that your gut[ix] is the main factor influencing your decision-making: survival, identity, protection, stimulus response, and fight or flight.

Do any of the above sound familiar?

Each brain has prime functions:

Head: cognitive perception, thinking and making meaning
Heart: emoting, values and relational affect
Gut: core identity, self-preservation and mobilization

Please note: Some of the functions of the three brains do crossover, the above definitions focus on the "prime" functions of each.

As well as prime functions, each brain also has a dominant expression:

Head: creativity
Heart: compassion
Gut: courage

There are times when these three intelligences are in conflict, or one is trying to do the job of another. You might recognize times when your head or gut is saying one thing and your heart is saying the opposite. For example, maybe you have a gut instinct that someone is bad for you, and yet your heart really wants you to be with that person and keeps you in a relationship.

When these intelligences are in conflict, you can find that you make bad decisions, or no decision at all.

What happens when we use one brain to do the job that another is designed for? For example, what happens if your head brain tells you who you should be in a romantic relationship with and you exclude your heart brain from the process?

What could happen if you align your three brains so that they work together?

With mBIT and my31Practices you can do exactly that.

THE AUTONOMIC NERVOUS SYSTEM

We have an autonomic nervous system (ANS) that is responsible for key functions in the body, such as regulating our breathing, heart beat and so on. The ANS is divided into two branches, the sympathetic and parasympathetic. Unlike its name suggests, the sympathetic ANS is about survival, and stimulus-response, fight or flight reactions to deal with stress and perceived danger. The parasympathetic system is responsible for rest and digestive processes. The two systems balance each other so you do not spend too much time in either; you are only in one or the other when necessary. Imagine what would happen if you spent most of your time in a fight or flight state. You would soon burn yourself out. This system of restoring balance is known as homeostasis.

PREPARATION

Before aligning your three brains, it is important to ensure that you are not operating from ANS sympathetic or parasympathetic polarities. Ideally you want to be balanced between the two, a state known as coherence, in order to avoid ANS bias.

BALANCED BREATHING

One of the fastest ways to get into coherence is through balanced breathing. The steps for this are outlined below:

1. Sit comfortably without any crossed limbs.

2. Breathe in deeply for a count of five or six beats (whichever feels more natural to you) and then out for the same number of beats.

3. Repeat this for about 2–3 minutes.

Tip: To get into the highest form of coherence, think of something that you find empowering; something that fills you with positivity or love or compassion. The beneficial results of these thoughts, alongside relaxed breathing can be seen when measured by a heart-rate monitor.

In what contexts would we want our three brains to be aligned?

There are nine broad contexts[x] where aligning the three brains can be practical, useful, and applicable to my31Practices:

1. Goal setting
2. Decision-making
3. Problem solving
4. Motivation and taking action
5. Harnessing your intuition
6. Cultivating understanding and perspective
7. Relationships
8. Personal development
9. Health and wellbeing

THE MBIT ROADMAP

The mBIT Roadmap is a process to establish communication with your three brains: align them so each is fulfilling its prime function, ensure that each is operating from its highest expression, and apply that highest expression for greater wisdom.

THE MBIT ROADMAP
- in practice

There are six steps to the roadmap:

1. **Discovery:** Decide what myValue or myPractice you want more insight into, where you are with that at present (perhaps what you currently do), and what is stopping you from expressing that more fully, achieving

whatever that is. Maybe it doesn't feel right, your heart's not in it, it doesn't make sense, you've had a belly full of trying that.

2. **ANS coherence:** Carry out the balanced breathing technique. You will make better choices for your myValues and myPractices.

3. **Communication:** Communicate with each brain in turn: As you continue balanced breathing, imagine breathing into your heart and connect with it. Ask the heart if it has anything to tell you regarding your myValue or myPractice. When you have an answer, imagine breathing into your head. Ask the head brain if it has anything to communicate. Once you have your answers, breathe deeply into your gut brain. Repeat the question.

4. **Congruence:** Align each brain by focusing on their primal functions using the mBIT foundational sequence of heart -> head -> heart -> gut -> heart. Start at the heart and ask the heart what it "truly wants" in relation to your myValue or myPractice. Then move up to your head, bringing the heart information with you. Ask the head what it "really thinks", including about what the heart truly wants. When you have your answer, move back to the heart. Sense the combined information from these two brains. Now move down to the gut brain bringing the heart and head information with you. Ask what the gut "deeply needs" in relation to your myValue or myPractice, with the information from head and heart in mind. When you

have your answers, move back to the heart and assimilate all the information.

Tip: Take your time with this process, fully associate to each step and seek to explore and be open to any thoughts that may come to you.

5. **Highest Expression:** Connect with each brain in turn once again and this time ask it to reveal its highest expression in relation your myValue or myPractice. Explore the use of metaphors (see Chapter 8 *Metaphor*) and symbology to help each brain find its highest expression – remember that the highest expression of the heart is compassion, the head is creativity and the gut is courage. Do this in the foundational sequence as before, heart -> head -> heart -> gut -> heart. Take your time to ask each brain to connect with its highest expression. As you move through each, assimilate the information collectively.

6. **Wisdom:** Future pace: Ask how the three brains are going to work together to produce the most ecological outcome for your myValue or myPractice based on the journey you have just taken. Ensure they are all aligned and working together.

Please note: If you experience constraints and/or blocks in finding alignment in using this process, mBIT has processes that can assist in dealing with this.

MBIT
and my31Practices

mBIT seeks to invoke the highest expression of your authentic self through alignment of head, heart and gut; through your thoughts, feelings, values and sense of identity. This is closely aligned with the my31Practices approach so the mBIT Roadmap might help you to draw on your three brains in developing your my31Practices. This will result in a set of myValues and myPractices which you feel comfortable with, with and you believe in, so they will have a greater chance of sustained success. Of course, you will still be able to fine-tune your myPractices as you start practicing them.

A number of factors can indicate that you are not in alignment; perhaps some of these have influenced you using the my31Practices approach and methodology. It could be that you sense internal conflict – perhaps you find yourself procrastinating from time-to-time as a result. Maybe you are not achieving what you believe you can. Maybe you just find yourself getting frustrated or angry. Do any of these sound familiar?

PAUSE FOR THOUGHT ...

How will you use mBIT to help you explore and get the most out of just one aspect of the my31Practices approach?

WANT TO KNOW MORE?

http://www.my31practices.com/the-book/resources/chapter-21

GOALS

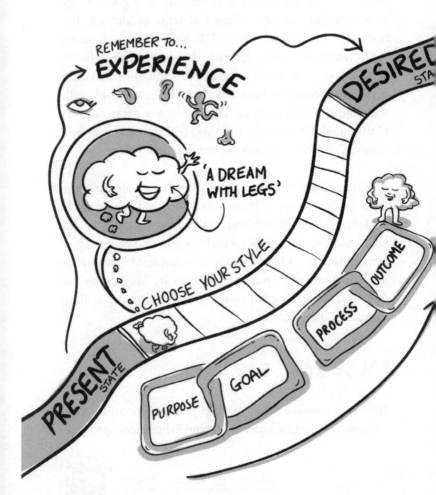

"A goal properly set is halfway reached."
Zig Ziglar[i]

A goal is a dream with legs.[ii] There is motion involved in a goal; action that takes you forward. At a simple level, there is where we are and where we want to be. In the field of neuro-linguistic programming (NLP) this is usually expressed as a present state and a desired state.

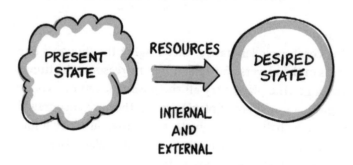

Figure 13. Present State to Desired State

We believe that for the goal to have the best chance for success, which can be more than just the completion of the task, it needs to be connected to purpose (why) and the style (how), drawing on the work of Simon Sinek's Golden Circle.[iii] The area of values, the my31Practices approach, and this book are more about your way of being or, in other words, the style.

To demonstrate, consider this example:

There are two coaches for children's soccer teams A and B playing in a league, and striving to get the best from their sides. What is their goal? At one level it might be to produce the best results. Win matches and win the league.

Team A
The coach uses a strict and directive approach, telling the players what to do and strictly enforcing this. The players play in the same positions week in, week out, so they become accomplished in their roles. The players with the best ability play the whole match and are told they need to do whatever it takes to win the game. The team wins all of its matches.

Team B
The coach is collaborative, encouraging the thoughts and ideas of the players and explaining the reasons why things are done. The players try all the positions and everybody is given a fair share of playing time. They are encouraged to pass the ball to a team mate, rather than just kick it forward, even when this might lead to mistakes. The team wins some matches and loses others.

At the end of the season, Team A has won the league and on one level, achieved their goal. However, Team B, despite not winning the league, benefited from learning how to play the sport and develop individually and as a team, learning about the importance of adaptability, social interaction, interdependence and mutual appreciation. And which coach would be happier? The answer is perhaps not as straight forward as you think – it depends on their values.

Often, it is the style in which you achieve your goal that might lead to a greater sense of fulfilment. Ideally, you are able to achieve the goal in the way that fits with your values. We have two questions for you: Would you rather be the coach for Team A or Team B? – and why?

As Figure 13 (page 247) shows, to get from one place to the other, we need resources. These resources can be either internal (e.g. resilience, confidence, passion) or external (e.g. time, money, sponsorship).

Setting goals is one thing, achieving them can be quite another. What is the difference between success and so-called failure? If you can identify the difference that will help you achieve a goal, then you stand a greater chance of increasing the likelihood of success.

There can be many reasons why goals do not come to fruition, for example, it could be that the goal is too big, too complex, impossible, not worth the effort, set for you and not really "yours", too time consuming, or too low down your list of priorities. Making sure you approach the goal from the strongest position can make all the difference. If you do not take sufficient care with the way you go about setting and achieving your goals, the end result can be, at best, ineffective and even counter-productive.[iv]

Your 31 myPractices represent the way you have chosen to bring to life your core values. They are how you want to behave. You can view them as 31 "goals" that you have set yourself. Importantly, the myPractices are easy to do, taking little effort and time, and you practice them every day.

This creates a system, or process goal, and increases your chances of happiness in the long run.[v]

So, how can you turn these myPractices into reality in the most effective way?

NLP has many tools and techniques for working with successful goal setting. One simple process you can use for each of your myPractices is referred to in NLP as "Well Formed Outcomes/Goals."

Before we look at the elements of a well-formed goal, it is useful to break goals into two categories:

1. Outcome Goal: The desired result.
2. Process Goal: The steps along the journey towards the desired result, often referred to as the plan or strategy.

With my31Practices, the main focus is on process goals, the strategy you employ, the way you do things.

STRATEGIES AND GOALS

"Our goals can only be reached through a vehicle of a plan, in which we must fervently believe, and upon which we must vigorously act. There is no other route to success."
Pablo Picasso[vi]

One way to increase the chance of achieving a goal is to state clearly what the goal is.

Research by psychologists Edwin Locke and Gary Latham suggests that people who articulate their goals boost their performance by 15%. This is with goals where results can be measured.[vii]

A strategy is a logical sequence that involves internal processing and external action to bring about a desired result. Everything you do involves a strategy, from deciding what to wear in the morning to making a cup of tea; from identifying your myValues to deciding your myPractices. A goal needs an effective strategy and the more well-formed that strategy is, the greater the chance of success.

To understand a simple strategy in action, imagine that your myPractice is to eat healthy food and you are sitting in a restaurant about to order. When you pick up the menu, what strategy do you run to choose a healthy meal? Do you also run a check to see what mood you are in, or look at certain dishes then imagine what they look like? Perhaps you imagine the taste and texture of the food and run a check to see if that feels right? If it does feel right, do you choose the dish or place it on a short list so you can run the same process for other items on the menu? You may even make a decision and then ask yourself what if this dish is not as healthy as your friend's dish, will you get food envy? You may even ask the other person if they are willing to share some of their dish with you so that you don't miss out. We have to run some form of strategy to make a decision.

When you are practicing your myPractices, be aware of the steps in your strategy for the best chance of success.

When your strategies are not working, you can improve your outcomes by exploring exactly why the strategy is not helping, make adjustments, and run the strategy again to see if you get a more desirable outcome.

An example of an unsuccessful strategy that you might have been running could involve seeing a delicious (but high calorie) meal and imagining how good it would feel to eat it. This feeling could be powerful enough to tempt you to order that dish. However, if you are aware that strategy doesn't bring you what you want, you could install a new step, such as at the moment you see the tempting dish, you immediately remind yourself of your myPractice "I eat healthy food" and ask the question: "Do I really want to consume that many calories?". This change of strategy could be all you need to behave in line with what is important to you.

You can use the same process to improve the strategies you are using for your myPractices.

There is a process in the NLP toolkit that is effectively a checklist or conditions that can act as a type of MOT[viii] or health check, ensuring that all the elements are functioning in the way that they need to for your goal to run smoothly.

WELL-FORMED OUTCOMES

Well-formed Outcomes in NLP are outcomes that satisfy certain conditions (listed below) and, when met, bring about the best chance of achieving success. When you are setting your myPractices goals, see if they meet the following conditions:

1. **Stated as a towards goal:**

   A positively motivated goal "towards" myPractice: I keep in touch with people I care about.

   Now let's look at the same myPractice, except that this time it is expressed in a manner that is not well-formed and does not move you towards a tangible and measurable progress goal. A negatively motivated goal "away from" myPractice: I don't want to lose touch with people I care for.

   The principle of stating your myPractice as a process and towards goal is also referred to in Chapter 9 *Affirmation*.

2. **That you know "why it is important" to you:**[ix]

   The my31Practices process ensures that your myPractices are appropriate and important to you. They are the myPractices you have chosen to demonstrate your myValues – in practice. This is a key factor because goals which are not so important to you may lose momentum when you start to encounter obstacles.

   When things get tough, it is your resilience that drives you on, and resilience comes from motivation, which is directly related to your values – what is deeply important to you.

3. **That you can associate with and sense all the steps involved in the goal:**

   You are a sensory being, you experience and re-experience the world through your five senses. When you set a goal for yourself, it is important that you can "see" yourself achieving the goal, "feel" what it would be like to achieve it and "hear" what you might hear when you achieve it.

If your myPractice is that you listen more effectively to others, your achievement comes from how you feel when you sense the effect your listening has on other people, when you discover new things in what others have to say, what you feel like when you notice others responding more positively, and you have more rapport with them. It is this sensory awareness that will resonate with and motivate you towards successfully implementing your myPractice. The same sensations will also provide the feedback to tell you that you are on the "right track".

This sensory feedback is often tacit; it can be a "gut" instinct (see Chapter 21 *mBIT*).

THE RETICULAR ACTIVATING SYSTEM (RAS)

The RAS is an area at the stem of the brain that provides, among many other things, a kind of sorting office function to keep your focus on what is important to you. You can programme your RAS by focusing on what you want, which places it high on the RAS list of priority. The more you focus on something, the more your RAS will direct your attention to it.

The RAS links directly with the my31Practices process of having a quote, a picture, and a video attached to your myPractice (see Chapter 13 *Reinforcement*). The more you see, hear and feel about your goal, the more you will be aware of anything related to it. An example of this is when you want to buy something; suddenly you see that something everywhere, a type of car for example, or a dress, or perhaps even a type of food.

This is why visualization boards are such a popular tool in self-coaching; it is the constant reminder of what you want that programmes the RAS.

The RAS is strongly linked with the Law of Attraction.[x]

4. **There are many options available to achieve your myPractice:**
   The more flexible you are and the more ways of achieving what you want, the greater the chance of success (see Chapter 17 *Presuppositions*).

   If your myPractice is to keep in touch, then you can do this by phone, email, text, in person, and so on. You have flexibility within your goal.

5. **The steps are simple and easily accomplished:**
   A key principle of my31Practices is that the myPractices are designed to be small steps in the service of a value – simple and easy to do.

   > *"Everything should be made as simple*
   > *as possible, but not simpler."*
   > — *Albert Einstein*[xi]

Beginnings are important because they provide the momentum to keep moving forward; therefore it is important to ensure that you break your goal down into manageable and achievable steps. As the first step begins the process, it is vital that it is clearly defined and something you can comfortably do. After the first step you will move to the next step. At this stage, the next step effectively becomes your new "first step".

6. **The myPractice adds to your life, it increases your choices:**
Having your myValues and myPractices in place and practicing them adds to your life and sense of alignment because they are an expression of your most important values. You are aware of the direct connection between your practical day-to-day behaviour and what is deeply important to you.

7. **Is your myPractice ecological?**
How does your myPractice affect you and those around you? All change or goals need to be checked for ecology in order to ensure that there are no unintended negative consequences from making that change (see Chapter 15 *NLP*). This is a guiding principle in NLP and other areas such as coaching and therapy-related practices. Have you checked your myPractices for ecology?

AN ECOLOGY CHECK
and my3lPractices

As a percentage, how much do you want this goal? If your answer is less than a 100%, ask yourself what stops it from being 100%.

What would happen if you achieved it?

What wouldn't happen if you achieved it?

What would happen if you didn't achieve it?

What wouldn't happen if you didn't achieve it? – Bear with this question; it is designed to make you think.

PAUSE FOR THOUGHT ...

How closely do your myPractices meet the well-formed conditions?

WANT TO KNOW MORE?

http://www.my31practices.com/the-book/resources/chapter-22

PART 4

STORIES

When we were thinking about the content of the book, we thought that you would be interested to hear from some people who have put the my31Practices approach and www.my31Practices.com into practice.

We invited a group of people to use the approach, keep a record of how they felt about it at various stages and then write a short story about their experience. We gave an outline structure for the story consisting of the person's background, what drew them to my31Practices initially, and an overview of their experience. You will see from the stories, however, that the individual style is very different.

From the stories submitted, we have chosen a selection and hope that Chapters 23–28 touch on topics and feelings that you might have: hopes, aspirations, questions, concerns, reservations. We have representation from the Caribbean, the UK, Australia and mainland Europe. We start with a perspective from a professional who uses values as a basis for her personal coaching business in Chapter 23 *Coach*. Then we have five personal stories in chapters 24–28, starting with one from co-author Alan. You can see the values chosen by these people and also their favourite quotation – including some from famous people you might have heard before, some attributed to family ancestors and even an original one!

We are very grateful to everybody who submitted their my31Practices stories and to thank the authors of those featured, they will share in the royalties received for the book. We trust that you will find the stories we have chosen to be an interesting collection written by real people around the world from very different walks of life.

COACH

"Vision without action is just a dream; action without vision just passes the time; vision with action can change the world."
Joel A Barker[i]

My name is Lindsay and I first heard about my31Practices at a UK Values Alliance presentation on the benefits of living your values every day. It was such a good fit with the Alliance's aim, "to put values at the heart of UK society", and with my own business that I wanted to find out more.

ME

I started using the my31Practices web application and chose five of my core ten values that I wanted to focus on and enhance in my day-to-day behaviours. I entered the specific things I wanted to do more of, and that was it. So simple, I loved it.

Every day I receive an email to remind me of my chosen value and the behaviour to focus on. It's one email, among the hundreds I receive that I actually look forward to, because it keeps me focused on what's important to me, rather than what matters to everyone else. It is a little uncanny, spooky even, how, during a challenging day, when the myPractice email pops up in my inbox it is often exactly the action I need to take to solve things and improve my day!

I remember one day when I'd been feeling a little low and the myPractice email that arrived said: "Kindness: get in touch with a friend" so I scanned through my contacts to find a friend who I hadn't seen for a while. I then sent her a text to see if she was free for lunch; she was so pleased I'd got in touch, we met the next day. She arrived with a beautiful bunch of flowers, so living my own value of kindness to others created an opportunity for that kindness to be reciprocated which made me feel energized and so much happier.

MY TEAM

So, as I use the my31Practices approach to help me live my values every day, and it really keeps me focused, I thought it would be great to share it with the team. I have trained many other coaches in my values-based coaching approach, so I signed up some of them to try my31Practices and also offer it to their clients.

In the courses I run, qualified coaches are trained in how to support their clients through a deep exploration of their values, to identify their top ten core values. These core values are then prioritized and measured in terms of how closely the individual is currently living their life aligned to those values and which ones they want to enhance.

The my31Practices approach is perfect to use as the next step after this exploration, as specific core values have been identified which can be immediately entered into the "myHub".

Specific behaviours identified through the coaching process, that the coaching clients want to do more of, can be entered as myPractices. They will then get a reminder to focus on one of their values each day. This also helps to bridge the gap between coaching sessions and supports achievement of progress.

Here's one that helped me. I'd been putting off following up with a potential client, concerned about being perceived as hassling them, as they hadn't replied to my last email. A myPractice email appeared in my inbox with today's action being "success: take a step towards success today", so I was motivated to send that email and within an hour they'd contacted me to arrange a meeting. They were happy I'd got in touch, they'd been meaning to reply to me but hadn't got around to it. Taking action to honour this value rather than listen to that fear or worry, doubled the feeling of success from gaining that client.

MY CLIENTS

As adults, our values are well-formed and won't change much throughout the rest of our lives, so focusing on aligning our behaviour to our values is a very sustainable approach. My clients come for coaching for many different reasons; the one thing they have in common is that they want to feel happier. Our values are what matters most to us, so honouring our values in our daily lives, through the decisions we make and the action we take, ensures that we will feel happier and more fulfilled as a result.

I now offer www.my31Practices.com as part of my coaching packages to clients as it is such a great way to help them to embed their chosen, values-based behaviours in daily life and supports them long after their coaching programme has finished. Using the my31Practices approach allows clients to measure and track progress. It provides a simple reminder each day to keep them focused and supports them in living their life aligned to what is truly important to them.

WANT TO KNOW MORE?

http://www.my31practices.com/the-book/resources/chapter-23

PRACTITIONER

"Even the Rolling Stones practice."
Alan Williams

My name is Alan and I created and developed the my 31Practices concept into what it is today.

Thinking about what to write for this piece made me wonder when my first version of the personal 31Practices was. It was a surprise to see the creation date on the Word document –17 November 2010. Of course, this was before www.my31Practices.com existed and I carried an A4 print out of the 31Practices in my pocket for easy reference each day. I have been practicing my31Practices ever since.

Two separate stories when put together demonstrate to me, and perhaps to you, the power of my31Practices:

I had visited a colleague at his office in London and told him about the idea to develop a personal application of 31Practices. To explain the idea to him, I used the example of somebody with a personal value of "compassion" and how the practice "I offer help to strangers who need it" could bring the value to life in a practical way. After the meeting, I was walking to the next appointment when I noticed an old lady on her own on the concourse at Victoria station. She then opened her purse too quickly and coins tumbled out, falling on the floor and rolling every-where. The station was busy with lots of people, I was in a hurry to be on time for the next meeting, and yet, against this backdrop of "busyness", I noticed this stranger who needed help. I did not think twice about going to assist. As I handed her coins back to her, she said, "I'm on a pension, love. Can't afford to throw it away," in a broad Cockney accent and laughed. It was only a short interaction and I remember walking away feeling energized.

A few weeks later, on a packed carriage on the London Underground, I was squashed, standing by the train doors. At the next stop, the doors on my side opened. A passen-ger left the train and somehow his rucksack caught the earphones of another passenger and took them with him. My eyes met those of the earphones owner across the crowded carriage, his face a picture of disappointment and resignation. The train doors closed, but the train did not move. Then the doors opened again. I happened to look down and, there on the platform, were the earphones. I stepped off the train, picked them up, stepped back on again, and passed the earphones to their owner. His face lit up and he gave me a "thumbs up". Neither of us said anything. I smiled inside for the rest of the journey.

To this day, and for evermore, a number of questions will remain unanswered: Why did I notice the old lady and then choose to help her? Was it anything to do with using an example of my compassion personal value, and having helping a stranger at the front of mind? Similarly, why did I notice the earphones being caught by the rucksack and then again lying on the platform? Why did I decide to pick them up to return them to their owner? Would this have happened if it had not been for the incident with the lady and her purse?

What I do know is that offering help to strangers has become "normal" behaviour for me, whether this is offering to carry a bag up or down stairs, giving directions to tourists, or returning a dropped newspaper. And the irony is this is not even one of myPractices.

One of the challenges with using the printed version was that I sometimes forgot to look at it. So one of the key functions for the www.my31practices.com web application was to use prompts at both ends of the day. I find this very useful to encourage me to know what the practice is at the beginning of the day and then again to think back on what I have done at the end of the day. I am improving at how often I look at the quote, picture and video clip chosen to reinforce the myPractice and really enjoy these few minutes of deeper "connection" with the practice. What difference does it make? For me, it's this thing about being more "front of mind" and putting it into practice somehow seems to happen more easily.

Another feature I find really useful is the measurement one. The way I use this is just as an indicator. I do not pour slavishly over the results, identify where I should do better and create an action plan. Instead, I complete the daily ratings just to have some form of assessment of how I thought I had done. As with all the other features, this will be used in different ways by different people and, ultimately, it will work best when you find your own way rather than use it in a prescribed way.

my31Practices has now become an established part of my daily routine, just as much as having a shower or brushing teeth. There are still days when I give it less attention than I would like but, when this happens, I recognize it and try to do better the next day. Overall, it helps guide me to behave in line with my values and make me aware that I am doing this.

WANT TO KNOW MORE?

http://www.my31practices.com/the-book/resources/chapter-24

TRAVELLER

"Big things are accomplished by starting with small things."
Muriël Robert
(inspired by Vincent Van Gogh[i] and Nelson Mandela[ii])

My name is Muriël and I was born in 1990, the year of German reunification, Nirvana and Nelson Mandela's release from prison. It was also the year that boy bands sounded through the radios and Will Smith was making us laugh in the *Fresh Prince of Bel-Air*. I live in Belgium, somewhere in the countryside, and not far from the city of Antwerp. Travelling, listening to music, and playing softball are my favourite spare time activities. I work full time for a facilities management company and my partner and I have a house remodelling/rebuilding project running – a second full-time job.

I was driven to participate in my31Practices because I was curious about how this change in behaviour could affect my daily life. "Be the best I can be" was a slogan that triggered my attention in the current busy times.

DISCOVERER

At first, it was very difficult to discover my true values. It took a little while because I came up with a long list of important values. To choose my top five core values from a long list was very difficult because it felt like *Sophie's Choice.* No better proof that I didn't know my true self and true values. I carried out several tests, did some self-reflection, and asked my family for their opinion. Eventually, I discovered my top values and started creating my daily practices.

During my31Practices, I had to attend a teambuilding event at work. It was about getting to know each other, reinforcing our collaboration, and improving the development of our services. During the event, we had to do a personality test, which showed our personal style and behaviour. The personality report corresponded to my personal values, so I knew I was on the right track. The two parallel exercises gave me a great insight of myself.

GO-GETTER

At a certain moment, I started doubting if the juice was worth the squeeze. It took quite some time and effort. But after a while, I was surprised at how many things I had done in the past 31 days. I have conducted activities/practices that I would never do on that particular day, because you always have excuses like "too busy", "too much work", other priorities, etc. Most of the time, I felt motivated when the myPractice of the day popped up and I felt energized by the outcomes.

For example, my value of the day was "fitness" and myPractice was: "I make time to practice sports in order to feel energized and fit!" I had just had an exhausting day. That morning I woke up with a terrible headache that

I had to endure the whole day. I had a lot of work and that evening I realized that I hadn't yet done myPractice of the day. I wasn't up for doing sports; I would rather finish some work and go to bed. Luckily I had added a fantastic quote and picture to my practice.

I looked at that picture again, knew that I couldn't cheat on myself and I went for a late-night run. Surprisingly, when I came home my headache was finally gone. I felt energized and went to bed with a great feeling. I felt refreshed and ready for the next day!

FIRST-BASE PLAYER

One weekend myValue was "success": to accomplish something noteworthy and admirable in my work and life. In general, doing it well and delivering excellence.

myPractices of the weekend were:

- I follow training, education and do research. I find ways to improve and develop myself.
- I try to understand everything and be able to do it. I don't give up, and finish what I started.

I was determined to carry out the myPractice well. I was taking part in a local softball tournament, playing against other teams. We had training together and feedback from the coaches, which was very interesting. I also did some research about softball and learned some new things. During the training I frequently asked players questions and received their feedback. After the game, I asked several questions, not only to my coach but also to our really experienced catcher, to try to improve as a first-base player. Actually, because of the myPractice, I learned so much more that day, more than in normal training and games. I came home exhausted, but I was proud that I didn't give up and attended both the teambuilding and softball that weekend. On Sunday night I was really impressed with what I had learned. I gave myself five stars on the myPractices rating.

"Mistakes are not a problem.
Not learning from them is."
Anon

After all, great things are done by a series of small things. This quote also reflects on my work. My team has been chosen as a finalist for an award, not for just one initiative but for a series of initiatives and best practices that we've carried out over time. Teamwork and perseverance are the key elements that have driven us to service excellence. Fingers crossed that we win the award! Editor's note: They did!

NATURE ADMIRER

For me, the value "fitness" means: "To practice self-awareness and healthy living in order to have physical and emotional wellbeing, the importance of being fit and feeling vitalized by doing sports." Sometimes I need more than sports and one of myPractices is: "I go to a quiet place to experience a sense of marvel through the exploration of nature." I knew that I really enjoyed doing this but it was a long time since I had chosen to do it. On one very busy day, I forced myself to go to a quiet place in nature, even though I didn't have time to go far.

When I was sitting in that nice place, not far from our home enjoying nature, I realized that I had been missing these moments. I had forgotten how relaxed it made me feel. A few years ago I lived in Switzerland for six months, and I did this all the time. I cleared my head by walking to the nearby lake and explored the mountains. It was not only about skiing or hiking, but also about just sitting on a rock on top of a mountain and admiring nature and "hanging loose". I remember coming home completely relaxed, all worries were gone. I had the energy to go on. It was a very important moment in my life, as I had experienced very difficult times. Switzerland changed me, and when I came home that night after myPractice, I realized I had that feeling that I had been missing for so long. My partner even noticed that I was more relaxed.

In spite of the busy times, I frequently think of this myPractice and practice it again. Even when it's just for five minutes, I walk in my garden to enjoy nature around me, or I look up to the stars.

After this experience, I have convinced my partner to go on holiday again this year. We've planned a trip to Croatia to tour and explore nature. This is important for me in order to feel energized to continue with everyday life.

"MY31PRACTICER"

The my31Practices approach has helped me to understand my priorities and find the true me. I feel energized and motivated to act more like who I truly am. The visual aspect of the my31Practices application makes it very easy, fun and engaging to do. I have been surprised at how much I have done. I am happy with the result and frequently repeat some myPractices, or at least keep them at the front of my mind. Actually, when I know I will need a particular myPractice, I add it in my agenda together with a quote and picture. I use them a lot.

WANT TO KNOW MORE?

http://www.my31practices.com/the-book/resources/chapter-25

"Your beliefs become your thoughts,
Your thoughts become your words,
Your words become your actions,
Your actions become your habits,
Your habits become your values,
Your values become your destiny."
Mahatma Gandhi[i]

My name is Amanda. I head up charitable organization Talent Match Staffordshire that helps people aged 18-24 not in education, employment, or training, into employment. I have a committed team of epic staff and volunteer teams who empower and enable our beneficiaries, and bring about wholescale changes to improve people's lives.

As a leader, being close to my values is critical to the success of the project and, more importantly, our beneficiaries. After several people I respect asked me why our project was doing so well where others had found difficulty, I began to look closely at the way we work. My mentor asked me if I had looked at my values, which, if I'm honest, I looked at after she had nudged me a number of times. We then went on to look at our values in Talent Match as a project, and in the people our services helps. So we learned the differentiator for us – our values!

I'm pretty busy – my workload is high and often unpredictable. Perhaps if I worked a 20-hour day I could achieve everything, but that's not practical. Was it a good idea to take part in my31Practices? I had no option, I couldn't work any harder, I had to work smarter. I used my31Practices to focus on what's really important. It was a little bit like clearing the windscreen of your car when it's covered in raindrops; you can kind of see where you're going but the rain drops are distracting. So, for the first time, I could clearly see the way forward and it felt good. It took just a few minutes, but saved me hours. It saved me from stress at work and I found leading the team became surprisingly simpler.

Initially, I did have to think and plan for the day, which is never a bad thing, rather than just wading in. However, just a few days in, it was becoming second nature and I didn't have to think about it much at all. I like the addition of images and enjoyed looking back at what I'd achieved, however, the most important difference was in me and my leadership. When my team saw me making choices linked directly to my values, they followed suit. The outcomes for our beneficiaries increased further and we remain a very productive team allowing young people to make big changes for their future. This has been an immediate boost for Talent Match, and will go on to have a long-term impact on the beneficiaries and organizations we work with. We openly talk about values with our young people and partners and encourage others to consider theirs too.

I now also use my values at home; motivating without the nagging. If my teenage children see my behaviours and positive thinking, it seems to inspire them to act similarly. Quite a surprise really!

I have found my31Practices to be a simple tool to motivate and improve both my work and home life. If someone had said that to me beforehand, I might not have believed them – it's like being on a speedboat with the waves parting for you!

WANT TO KNOW MORE?

http://www.my31practices.com/the-book/resources/chapter-26

CHANGEMAKER

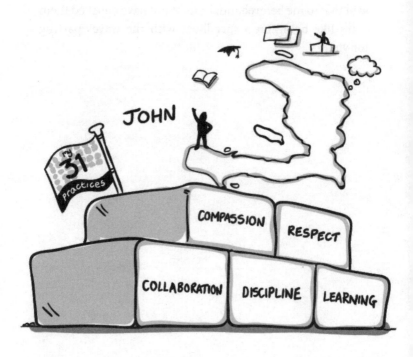

"Keep on, keepin' on."
Jacob Martin Engle (my grandfather who lived to 93)

My name is John Engle and I'm a co-founder and co-director of Haiti Partners. Haiti Partners' mission is to help Haitians change Haiti through education. There are 1,200 students in our schools and we have a flagship school, the Children's Academy and Learning Center, where we're developing a "Changemaker Education" model. The model comprises as a central element, community development and life-long learning. We're also providing scholarships to 35 Haitians attending Haiti-based colleges and equipping them to be child and women's rights activists. In May 2013, I received a Lifetime Achievement Award from WorldBlu for my work in Haiti promoting democratic practice and freedom-centred leadership. I live in Haiti with my wife Merline and two children.

I LOVE MY31PRACTICES!

What I've benefited tremendously from is reviewing, every single day, the myPractice for that day. I love this daily habit. I love that my31Practices required me to invest time and energy to articulate, very succinctly, 31 separate practices that would help me become more who I wanted to be. Then, every single day I focus on one of these, think about it and take action when I see an opportunity. I'm reminded of the practice that I established and at the end of each day, I reflect on how I have integrated it and the impact it has had. Here are several concrete examples of how my31Practices is helping me become more of whom I want to be:

1. I've reduced my sugar intake and am eating really well – lots of fruits and vegetables. I have lost 10 pounds since December and have kept it off. I feel great!

2. I've stopped drinking alcohol. I know that my31Practices has helped me stay strong and liberated. It helped me get through the holidays in December, which would normally be a time when alcohol would be a big part of my celebrations.

3. I've become better than I ever was at inviting co-workers and colleagues to think with me. I'm constantly asking myself, "This idea that I have and which I've begun acting on, who do I need to ask for advice about it? Who do I need to invite to think with me on it?"

I remember one day when myPractice was "I am alert to people who are not in a good mood and seek to understand why." It's like I had a reawakening. All of a sudden, the person in front of me became a human being with needs and hurts instead of just a Haitian government bureaucrat. My demeanour changed, we ended up joking and connecting on a human level. Instead of a moment that diminished both of us, through mutual frustration, it became a moment of connection, of warmth.

Whether it's taking more time and being more attentive to deep breathing, to listening to others, to allowing myself to feel the pain of others and develop more empathy, I'm growing. I typically use the end of a year to reflect about the past year and think ahead to goals for the upcoming year. The my31Practices approach has helped me get much more traction this year and has shaped the "way" I want to be. My next step is to use some of the other features, such as adding photos and videos and regularly rating my progress, which I think will help to embed my practices even further.

WANT TO KNOW MORE?

http://www.my31practices.com/the-book/resources/chapter-27

SEEKER

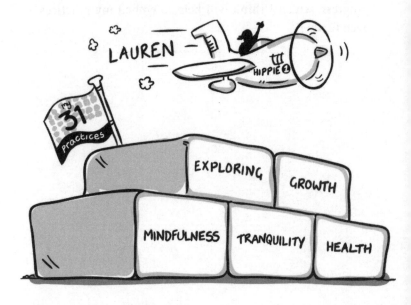

"When my circle got smaller, my vision got clearer."
Anonymous

I think it is important to express gratitude each and every day, and that's how I look at my life. My name is Lauren – I'm young, independent and live in one of the most beautiful places in the world, Queensland, Australia. I have been fortunate enough to balance travelling the world and working hard to have a successful career in aviation. I have been afforded many amazing professional opportunities which I believe have made me realize early on in my adult life that what is most important isn't my job title and my annual salary, it's my personal life that matters most. An epiphany many people don't seem to have until much later on in life. I like to think of myself as a business professional by day, and a New Age hippie on the weekends (I sound confused don't I?).

I have an open mind when it comes to learning new things. I'm always seeking out new ideas, new information and better ways of living, whether it's reading about self-awareness or practising meditation. I noticed that I was having more and more conversations about values and how they drive our behaviours. However, it wasn't until quite recently that I met someone who had found themselves in conflict with their values and the way they led their life. So what did they do? They moved towns, quit their job, and started working for themselves. This person challenged me on my values and whether I was honouring them in the way I behaved and lived my life.

So, how did I find myself on the my31Practices journey? Like many things these days, I first started following my31Practices on social media. It was the message about values that drew me in, "live your life by your core values and see where these will take you", how simple.

When I first started looking into my31Practices, I thought, "I cannot believe how simple this concept is, yet I don't do this every day, and I don't know anyone who does either," I was hooked.

When it came to setting the myPractices I was surprised at how much thought went into this. The myValues came easily, it was the daily practices to complement the values that I really had to think carefully about (and yes, maybe I Googled a thing or two, I mean c'mon who doesn't use Google for everything?). Looking back, the key was in making them practical and achievable, while still challenging, and not being afraid to go back and edit them. The other key was setting values that are important to me now, not values that might be important to me in the future. For example, family is incredibly important to me, however, I found that I am content in that area of my life and I chose values that I want to commit to practicing (e.g. mindfulness, tranquillity, etc.).

Looking back after a couple of months of practicing, I loved that my whole day didn't revolve around my daily practices, but that they were gentle reminders of my values, and during those long, difficult days we need these gentle reminders about what is truly important. my31Practices gave me new energy, I felt reinvigorated and committed to doing things in my life that align with my values. I found that where I had neglected myself over the past few months, due to work and stress, I was back committing to myself again and doing the things I love. Over time, completing my31Practices became second nature. Importantly, recording them daily with a small note made me accountable – at one point I "fell off the wagon" (technical error on my part) and I honestly had withdrawals. I found recording the my31Practices held me accountable and this made all the difference.

I have kept a diary since I started my my31Practices journey. When I first started I wrote, "My practices will just be things that come naturally to me." But now I'm finding myself acknowledging my myPractice and thinking, "Ok, how can I fulfil this today?" I am finding this refreshing. It's different, I feel productive and accomplished as I work through my daily practices.

So, what change did I notice in myself? I'm a little cynical so I was pleasantly surprised that I noticed and felt a significant change in my mood and temperament. At one point my diary notes, "Loving this person!" It was the little things that I was accomplishing through my practices that were making me feel motivated, a practice as simple as "do something to challenge yourself" had me running that little bit further than before. I remember when my practice was "try something new", I had been entertaining the idea of doing a meditation workshop for more than six months, and my practice helped me to finally make the decision to do it – it turned out to be an incredible six-week experience and has paved the way for my on-going meditation sessions.

Where I noticed the most significant change was with my overall value for "health", since I have started my31Practices I have become mainly vegetarian, a choice made for health reasons. I have made more time for yoga, planning my meals in advance, and eating more whole foods.

If I had to pick a favourite myPractice, it would be "show kindness, doing something nice for someone else", it may seem simple but I got an unexpected amount of joy from completing this. One practice in particular I remember was for no reason sending a close friend a nice message to say how proud I was of them.

Reflecting on where I was at the beginning of this journey, it was easy to believe that I could put a few values together and add a few practices to these; however, the reality for me was it was only through my31Practices that I found I actually honoured these. I think too often we get caught up in, "I'll do that soon", "I'll start that next week", but before we know it, Christmas has come around again like it was here last month.

I can honestly say that I could not have followed my practices without the practical approach of my31Practices.
Let's be honest, if I was still doing this myself it would
be six months down the track and I'd still be sorting out
my values.

WANT TO KNOW MORE?

http://www.my31practices.com/the-book/resources/chapter-28

PART 5

RECAP

If you are super-busy, with no time to read even this short, fast read action book, Chapter 29 summarizes the importance of "being you" in today's dynamic world and provides an overview of the six steps of how my31Practices helps you to achieve this, with further tips for you to consider. How to release the power of your values for authentic happiness, in a nutshell ...

RECAP

FRAMEWORK / METHODOLOGY

PURPOSE

FIND YOUR

CORE VALUES

BEING VS DOING

DAILY BEHAVIOURS

31 Practices

TAKE ACTION...

LIVE YOUR VALUES... EVERY DAY

LESS STRESSED

HAPPY

THE BEST VERSION OF YOU

AUTHENTIC HAPPINESS

"A journey of a thousand miles begins with a single step."
Lao Tzu[i]

So, you have reached the final chapter – or maybe this is your starting point to gain a quick dive into my31Practices! Whatever stage you are at as you read this chapter, we trust that you have found, or will find, our book enjoyable, stimulating, thought-provoking and helpful. Our best hope is that you will be inspired to do something different to be you, and that you will find your VALUES Superhero, or at least gain a glimpse. We will be delighted if you continue to revisit various chapters on a regular basis, not only to read the words we have written but also to try the activities, to add your own notes, thoughts, comments and questions, to explore some of the suggested resources and to practice what you have read about. So keep this book with you, or somewhere easily accessible.

As we mentioned in Chapter 1, the content we have written is powerless until you do something with it. But when you do take action, it can bring great power, as shown by the uplifting stories in Part Four. This is why we have created my31Practices as an action book for ongoing reference and use, rather than a one-time read.

The key context for people in general, whatever your walk of life, is that we all live in a dynamic world fuelled by speed, connection and change. The pace of life has never been quicker and continues to accelerate; it is a super-connected world where you can communicate a message in an instant – either to a specific individual or to millions of people. So much is changing all the time, sometimes radically and often very fast. This all makes for a complex environment to navigate.

But against this whirlwind landscape, you are still human with some basic and simple characteristics. You are an emotional being in need of a sense of purpose and a sense of what is important to you. These base needs are very powerful.

In the past, you might have been tempted to create an "image" for yourself, according to what you, or others, thought would work best for you. But work best for what? To perform a role? To run faster on the hedonic treadmill? How comfortable are you to play this "role"? How much energy does it take? What happens when the mask slips?

As the world becomes more dynamic, this image-fabrication approach is less and less relevant. It is more appropriate to be authentic. Why is this?

Consider this statement for a few seconds before you read on:

You are no longer what you say you are, but, instead, what other people say you are.

What does this say to you?

Perhaps you think it has rather negative connotations and you might be more in tune with this quote:

> *"Be more concerned with your character than your reputation, because your reputation is merely what others think you are."*
> *John Wooden[ii]*

Isn't it more important to focus on you, rather than how other people see you?

On the other hand, in light of the super-connected world in which we live, you will probably also agree with the sentiment of this quote:

> *"It takes many good deeds to build a good reputation, and only one bad one to lose it."*
> *Benjamin Franklin[iii]*

So, how can you balance this apparent contradiction between focusing on your character and your reputation?

We think we have some good news for you. What if it is not a case of choosing between a focus on yourself or on what other people think? What if there is just one single focus – being you?

Because you are so much more connected and visible, it is your real self that will show through, sooner or later, whether you want it to or not. So why not do this intentionally and excellently? Also, the more you are authentic, the more this will be visible in the world and the more it will be amplified because of the way modern communication works. You are in a better position to lead by example, be the example, and be the change, than you have ever been before – by being you. This applies whatever your circumstances and whatever your role: you might be a student or a C-suite executive, a member of a family or a community leader, a parent or a single adult, a public sector worker or a volunteer, a scientist or an athlete, a teacher or an artist. Whatever your circumstances and whatever your role, you can choose to lead and use my31Practices to be YOU.

Of course, values alignment is no mean feat, even at an individual level. You need to overcome the barriers of personal short-term interests, other people's demands and expectations, and balancing different commitments. You also need to do this consistently because any failure or shortfall may be communicated to millions in a flash. No mean feat indeed. You might think: "If it was easy to do, everybody would be doing it already," – but it becomes much easier to do when you know your values.

> *"When your values are clear to you, making decisions becomes easier."*
> *Roy E Disney[iv]*

Achieving values alignment in practice consists of just six simple steps:

1. Identify a set of core personal values (myValues) that are important to you (in support of your purpose) and be clear about what the values words mean to you.

2. Translate the values into practical behaviours (myPractices) – and have fun using metaphor to do this.

3. Write your myPractices in an affirmation style.

4. Reinforce your myPractices with a favourite photo, video and quote.

5. Consciously focus on a myPractice each day.

6. Reflect on your experiences at the end of each day, recognizing what worked well and what could be better next time. Try the scoring to see how this works for you and record your myExperiences.

We also have these ten tips for you to consider as you follow the six steps:

1. Make your myPractices specific enough so you will know when you have done them – ask the question "What does that look like?"

2. Allow yourself time to live with, adjust and refine your myValues and myPractices until you are happy with them – in all aspects of your life (personal, social and work).

3. Adopt and develop a curious, learning mindset, rather than focusing on the known.

4. Be alert and consciously seek out opportunities to practice.

5. Assess the impact of your behaviour on yourself and on other people. What happened because of what you did? What would have happened, or not happened, if you had not done this?

6. Proactively use your myValues to guide your decision-making.

7. Constantly refine your approach so that it continually improves.

8. Be aware of the underpinning psychological, sociological, and philosophical principles that are at play: heart, mind and body in alignment.

9. Recognize that you do not operate in a vacuum and that there is a broader system and context (ecology) in which you exist and live.

10. Make it your own personal approach – of course, you can learn from others but always apply these learnings to your own particular circumstances which are unique to you.

As you can see, this is very straightforward and is the very core of the my31Practices approach: on the one hand, simple and based on doing a little every day – on the other, requiring strong discipline and obsession with authentic delivery: every action, every day. Practice makes more perfect – keep practicing. Over time, the values become part of your daily conversation and embedded into the way you feel, think and behave every day. It becomes natural and you become congruent. You release the power of your values every day for authentic happiness.

You might remember we started this book with a quote from a Harry Potter book to introduce the first chapter, and we finish with another quote from a popular source which we think provides a highly contemporary endorsement of the my31Practices approach. Think personal branding from the inside out:

"Never forget what you are, for surely the world will not. Make it your strength. Then it can never be your weakness. Armour yourself in it, and it will never be used to hurt you."
George R R Martin, A Game of Thrones
(A Song of Ice and Fire, #1)

AND FINALLY

If you are interested in learning more about the history and ongoing developments of the original 31Practices approach and my31Practices, the final two chapters (30 *Beginning* and 31 *Present*) of the book provide this. And at the end of this book, we have put together a short quiz for you to enjoy!

PAUSE FOR THOUGHT ...

What have you seen so far of your VALUES Superhero?

WANT TO KNOW MORE?

http://www.my31practices.com/the-book/resources/chapter-29

PART 6

JOURNEY

With this part of the book we have followed the style of a number of more recent films and novels where the beginning is not at the beginning. Part 6 is a prequel that shares the 31Practices journey from the beginning, to provide a deeper insight into the background and development of the approach, as well as taking a look at developments and possibilities for 31Practices and my31Practices. Chapter 30 *Beginning* deals with the origination and evolution of the 31Practices approach and how the first *The 31 Practices* book came to be published; Chapter 31 *Present* considers the current and emerging agenda, with a look at what might be possible in the future.

BEGINNING

"From tiny acorns, mighty oak trees grow."
Anonymous

The my31Practices journey began some time ago – in fact, in the last century!

Hanbury Manor, a five-star Marriott hotel in the UK in 1999, provided the first inspiration and the initial principles upon which the original 31Practices approach was based and has been developed since.

The Ritz Carlton luxury-hotel chain developed their credo: "Ladies and gentlemen serving ladies and gentlemen". This offers a sense of purpose that all those serving the Ritz Carlton brand were asked to demonstrate by living a collection of service behaviours called "Daily Basics".

Ritz Carlton was a subsidiary of Marriott and the parent company adopted the "Daily Basics" routine in all Marriott hotels globally, where employees focused on one of 22 hospitality behaviours (or Basics) each day.

A number of performance milestones were achieved at Hanbury Manor between 1997 and 2002. Hanbury Manor received the most improved Associate (employee) opinion survey across Marriott hotels, globally; the most improved guest satisfaction survey in the UK; uniquely, "all green" balanced scorecard business measures for three consecutive years; and AA Hotel of the Year. The Daily Basics approach was a key tool enabling this success – it was the simplicity of a focus on one specific behaviour each day that had such a powerful impact.

APPLICATION

The principles of the Basics approach which had been applied so successfully to customer service were subsequently applied in the area of organizational values. Then, and still today, core values of organizations are often displayed in lobbies and boardrooms, but are not lived through employee behaviours. What if employees understood more explicitly how these values translated into day-to-day behaviour and were encouraged to practice them – every day?

It was at this stage that another small but important "tweak" happened. Because at Marriott there were 22 Daily Basics, there was no synchronization between the day of the month and the number of the Basic behaviour being applied. Although this sounds crazy, it did have a negative impact: one frustrated employee summed it up with: "I get confused when it is Basic 15 and it's only the 2nd of the month." A simple answer to this was to have 31 behaviours, as there are never more than 31 days in a month.

This is how the 31Practices approach was created – although not yet in name. The results were dramatic, delivering significant business impact and receiving client and industry awards.

"Knowledge is of no value unless you put it into practice."
Anton Chekhov[i]

DEVELOPMENT

ServiceBrand Global is a business coach and consultancy business started in 2005 to assist organizations with improving the quality and effectiveness of face-to-face service delivery. One of the first clients was a global investment bank that wanted to create a consistent culture and service standard in key locations globally.

At this time, the 31Practices name was created and it seemed to be appropriate because of the focus on "practicing" the value-linked behaviours on a daily basis. It was during this first project that the power of employee co-creation was also recognized. One employee from the post-room in the New York office of the investment bank said with pride "Look! Practice number 16! I suggested that in our workshop!"

Once live, organizations are encouraged to integrate the 31Practices approach with their recognition strategy enabling employees to nominate colleagues who they see displaying the Practices excellently – even nominating themselves. This works best when a non-management cross-functional group is responsible for selecting the best examples on a monthly basis.

Notably, employees play a co-creation role and take ownership for development of the way the tool is used. Employees are given the freedom to apply each daily practice at work as they wish.

To use an example of a hotel group, if the core value is "excellence" and today's Practice is, "We display meticulous attention to cleanliness," the receptionist might tidy a cupboard, the engineer might sweep the boiler room, the chef might book the de-greasing of the filters, etc. The organization's "heritage" is created through the communication of stories which positively reinforce the desired behaviours.

Finally, while the overall framework and principles of the 31Practices methodology are consistent, the specific details of the 31Practices are unique to each client organization.

The next stage of development was to consolidate the business proposition: develop the commercial model and the brand. 31Practices is a registered trademark with a distinctive logo. It is provided to client organizations on a subscription arrangement on the basis that the best impact from the approach is achieved when every employee applies each daily practice. A client recently told us: "I spend that much each year on uniforms to make sure my people look the part, so if this helps them behave right, it is great value." The eye-catching appeal of a uniformed employee is a good start, but employee behaviour being aligned with the values of the organization is much more fundamental and meaningful.

A leadership team event has been specifically included in the implementation phase to design and support the operating platform for 31Practices. How will the methodology be embedded into everyday processes such as interviews, induction, standard operating procedures, daily buzz meetings, recognition programmes and more?

Every organization is different and it is critical that 31Practices "fits", is owned, and that leaders feel accountable for the effective use of the framework. This powerful set-up process, together with planned reviews, keeps 31Practices fit for purpose, achievable, and effective.

More than ten years may seem a long time to develop what is, on the surface, a very simple tool, but perhaps this is its strength. The development has been grounded in practical application rather than management theory and books. 31Practices brings an organization's core values to life through the behaviour of every employee, every day. The approach helps instil a common culture across departments, supply-chain delivery partners and remote workers. Over time, consistency of behaviour is built through repetition. 31Practices has been used in a variety of local, national and international businesses and has played a major part in the measurable balanced scorecard success achieved in these businesses. A client project received the 2015 Employee Engagement Award from the Association of Business Psychology and the approach is now available on a licence basis for consultant practitioners to promote and deliver to their clients.

The core methodology above forms the underpinning principles of the my31Practices approach, but it is applied in an individual rather than organizational context.

"Life is really simple, but we insist on making it complicated."
Confucius[ii]

BOOK

"It's a bizarre but wonderful feeling, to arrive dead center of a target you didn't even know you were aiming for."
Lois McMaster Bujold[iii]

Here's the short version from Alan Williams of how the first book, *The 31 Practices: Release the Power of Your Organization's VALUES Every Day* came about:

"In 2011, I decided to seek out a qualified psychologist with a background in organizational psychology to collaborate with. This was because I knew that the 31Practices approach worked, but was not satisfied with this and curious to understand better why it worked, from a more academic, psychology perspective. Two people I had met that year in completely different ways suggested the same person, Alison Whybrow, a chartered psychologist and coach. In less than two years after making contact, the book *The 31 Practices* had been co-authored and published."

A summary of the book is as follows:

In our super-connected world, organizations' brands and reputations are shaped to a far greater extent by the personal experience of their employees and customers. We already know that 70% of customers, brand perception is determined by their experience with the organization's employees and 41% of customers are loyal due to employee attitude. Authenticity from the tip to the root is the new Holy Grail for organizations. This book shows how an organization's values and brand can be translated into the daily practices and behaviour of their employees, drawing a golden thread from the boardroom to the front-line customer experience. The 31Practices method weaves together principles and practices from psychology, sociology, philosophy, neuroscience, leadership and business to significantly enhance customer and employee satisfaction and loyalty. It has been successfully adopted by large and small companies, across sectors from around the world.

Certain "design principles" seemed intuitively "right": 31 chapters, a beautiful black and white photograph to introduce each chapter and reinforce the chapter title, one word chapter titles in keeping with the 31Practices core theme of simplicity, hardback format to emphasize "quality" and "substance".

"Do you think the universe fights for souls to be together? Some things are too strange and strong to be coincidences."
Emery Allen[iv]

The book is dedicated to "the alchemy of relationships, curiosity and serendipity" – and Alan recalls some of the examples of serendipity as the project developed.

Publication

"A colleague, Ian Ellwood, I had met some years before at an interview for a senior role at Interbrand offered a template for anybody writing a book synopsis saying that "it had never failed" and also recommended making contact with Martin Liu, LID Publishing. Martin liked the book concept and agreement was reached very quickly." The alchemy of ...

> *"I always leave room for serendipity and chance."*
> Ken Stott[v]

Photography

"The photography element was progressed courtesy of Google after a number of unproductive avenues. It was a Sunday afternoon "googling" a combination of psychology, happiness, practice, photography, etc. when suddenly up "popped" Matthieu Ricard: Buddhist monk, author on topics such as happiness and altruism, translator for the French government for the Dalai Lama – and photographer!! A quick email exchange with the people at Matthieu's foundation, Karuna-Shechen, resulted in an agreement to use his wonderful photographs in exchange for a donation to the Foundation. As a fitting epilogue to this sub plot, in September 2013, the people from Karuna-Shechen let us know that Matthieu was in Europe in October: would we like to meet him? The meeting took place on a warm, sunny day in a beautiful garden in the suburbs of Paris. Matthieu liked the book and endorsed it with a short video which we were proud to show at our book launch the following day, which was a pure coincidence." The alchemy of ...

Launch

"A colleague, Neil Usher, a workplace senior executive, had made an introduction to Mark Catchlove who is the Director, Insight Group for Herman Miller Ltd, the recognized innovator in contemporary interior furnishings. Mark liked the 31Practices concept and was generous enough to host the book launch at their very smart office showroom at Aldwych, London. Friends, family and colleagues gathered for a wonderful celebratory occasion." The alchemy of ... . Alan recalls "It was the first time somebody asked me to sign a copy of the book, and I thought they were joking!"

> *"What people call serendipity sometimes is just having your eyes open."*
> José Manuel Barroso[vi]

Circles

The final example is perhaps the most bizarre of all. Alan says: "Because the 31Practices journey started with inspiration from Ritz Carlton, it seemed fitting to honour this in some way. Horst Schulze had been the President and COO of Ritz Carlton at that time, so I approached him to endorse our book. A contact on LinkedIn, Chris Reed, Langham Hospitality, introduced me to Mr Schulze's PA and a few months later we were proud to feature this quote on the back cover of the book:

"The 31Practices approach is simple, clear, at times daring and unconventional to the traditional thinker of today. But this will be the norm and essential in the future. Good job – I really enjoyed it."
Horst Schulze, Chairman/CEO, Capella Hotel Group and ex-President/COO of Ritz-Carlton.

The alchemy of ...

"Hard work increases the probability of serendipity."
Ken Poirot[vii]

The UK launch in October 2013 was followed by the US launch in August 2014 and in 2015 publishing partnership arrangements were put in place in India and South Korea. It's been quite a journey and is still going strong!

SERENDIPITY
- in practice

What are your favourite personal stories of serendipity and what did you do or not do that allowed them to happen?

PAUSE FOR THOUGHT ...

What single moment was the beginning of your interest or curiosity in values?

WANT TO KNOW MORE?

http://www.my31practices.com/the-book/resources/chapter-30

PRESENT

"The future depends on what you do today."
Mahatma Gandhi[i]

As the concept of 31Practices for organizations was developing, the idea of how the same approach could be applied to help individuals was forming in parallel. It seemed logical to make use of technology and mobile phones somehow, to take advantage of the way most of us live our lives, and also to make it as accessible and user friendly as possible. What is the longest period of time you have which is "technology free"?

The search for a technology partner to design and build a my31Practices web application was not an easy one, mainly because many of the companies we came across were experts in technology but not so interested in creating a customer friendly tool. It took years to explore various alternative companies, slowly progressing the structure and features of the concept. You might not be surprised to hear that it was another personal connection and a "chance" encounter was involved. Fiona Anderson, a culture change and organizational design colleague, knew David Ohandjanian of ADAO Design through her daughter. David had been very helpful in setting up a charity website, so he also seemed to have a similar set of values. Fiona made the introduction.

David Mace, a connection of Alison Whybrow, assisted with translating the various features and functions of my31Practices into wireframes that could be used to build the specification. ADAO were one of three companies considered and were chosen because of their design and customer experience focus. Some nine months later, www.my31Practices.com was ready for beta testing and went live in its full form in 2015. When considering the price point, gym memberships were a benchmark. If people are willing to invest in achieving the physique they want, why not take the same approach for how you want to behave? It also seemed appropriate to reinforce the 31 theme and this is why the annual subscription is £31. If enough people sign up, perhaps this could become £0.31 at some point!

As we are writing this, some improvements to the site are being made and developed, focusing on mobile usability and feedback from people who have used www.my31Practices.com about how they would like to see it develop.

MEANWHILE ...

In the meantime, the 31Practices approach for organizations continued to go from strength to strength. In 2015 Alan and his client Tamsin Parker, Director of People and Culture for the independent life insurance provider LifeSearch, received the Association of Business Psychology Employee Engagement Award. In particular, the judges cited the remarkable business impact as being a main reason for their decision.

> *"The present moment is filled with joy and happiness.*
> *If you are attentive, you will see it."*
> Thích Nhất Hạnh[ii]

The 31Practices approach develops with each project, and recent successes have included the following:

- communication on a "social platform" using #31P to encourage discussion and sharing.
- an illustration competition to be featured on desk-top flipover calendars.
- the development of a corevaluescore survey to provide a snapshot of stakeholder perception of the degree to which the organization is living the stated values.
- advanced discussions are taking place with a number of organizations/people about building a network of licensed 31Practices Practitioners in various locations (Australia, India, Egypt, Phillipines, South Africa and South Korea). We are always interested to hear from people or organizations who may be interested to take part in this network.

WHAT'S NEXT? WHO KNOWS?

We have shared with you above some of the emerging ideas and intentions for both 31Practices and my31Practices but there is no "master business plan". Apologies if you are disappointed to read this! From the beginning of the 31Practices concept and all through its development, the approach has been one of organic evolution rather than a driven plan. Some people may point out that this has meant slower progress and success on a smaller scale than could have been achieved. This may, or may not, be true. What we do know is that it has been a stimulating, enjoyable and fulfilling journey for many people who have been involved in different ways and we look forward to more unknown developments in the coming months and years.

> *"True happiness is ... to enjoy the present,*
> *without anxious dependence upon the future."*
> Lucius Annaeus Seneca[iii]

FUTURE HISTORY

We are also able to share current future thoughts, some of which may be history by the time you are reading this book:

In your hands

You are holding one development in your hands with the *my31Practices* book. John, whose illustrations we hope you are enjoying throughout this book, helped with the whiteboard animation on www.my31Practices.com so it was an easy decision to invite him to take part in this project.

Steve, co-author, was another chance meeting. He is one of a few neuro-linguistic programming (NLP) Master trainers in the UK and was teaching a course in London. When we discussed the alignment between NLP and my31Practices, it was quickly apparent that this was a great combination to write a book – so that's what we decided to do, and 18 months later it has been published.

Values-driven community

Alan has founded the Global Values Alliance with a network of values-driven colleagues from all over the world and also continues to take part as a Steering Group member of UK Values Alliance (www.valuesalliance.co.uk). By the time you are reading this, you may have become aware of an inaugural World Values Day, www.worldvaluesday.com, being celebrated on 20 October 2016 – if you do not know anything about it, ask Mr Google what happened with this, and see how you can join in in 2017. As a reminder, to celebrate World Values Day in October 2016 and the publication of this book at the turn of the year, we are offering one year's subscription to www.my31Practices.com for a special price of £21. Just use the promotional code BEYOU2017 when you sign up before 31 January 2017. People have told us this is a great idea for a present.

Foundation course

The first Foundation Course took place June 2016. This is part of the familiarization process for organizations and potential licensed practitioners to learn about the 31Practices approach in detail before deciding to progress with implementation. We are seeking to build a network of licensed practitioners all over the world, so if you know anybody who is passionate about helping client organizations to create a values-driven environment in practice, and sees value in the 31Practices approach, let us know.

Retreat

You might be reading this book having attended our first my31Practices retreat in Marbella in November 2016. As we write this, we are curious to know what you thought, although by now you have probably had the chance to tell us! The my31Practices retreat is designed to provide focused time and attention in a relaxed environment with like-minded people. The objectives are:

- to be able to explain why and how the my31Practices approach works.
- to create your personal set of myValues and myPractices.
- to begin to explore how pictures, quotes, and videos can reinforce the approach.
- to practice your myPractices.
- to share your thoughts, feelings, and experiences in a supportive environment.
- to develop a positive mindset for your return to life/work.

We've also had some preliminary discussions about how we could add an additional layer, or layers, of value by this retreat becoming a regular activity where people who are on their my31Practices journey come together to share tools and techniques, new findings in neuroscience, and their personal experiences.

Employee benefit

In Chapter 19 *Alignment*, we touch on the importance of the workplace environment and values alignment. Employers are starting to recognize the benefits of this. Research shows that clarity about personal values delivers up to 17% commitment above the norm – clarity about personal values and organizational values delivers up to 19%. Interestingly, when people only have clarity about the organization's values this can have a slight negative impact, taking commitment 0.5% below the norm.[iv] We are having further discussions with employers who are considering providing my31Practices to their employees as a benefit of employment. It is certainly a very visible way to demonstrate a commitment to a values-driven approach, taking this beyond an organization-centric perspective to one providing support at an individual level as well.

Pass it on

As the www.my31Practices.com web application becomes more widely used, another element of the approach is that for every paid subscription, a free use will be given to a partner organization which sees value in this for people they work with. Our first partner is Haiti Partners https://haitipartners.org/, who you can read more about in Chapter 27 *Changemaker* and we are interested to hear from other organizations that might wish to join us in this way. However, in the short term, we are likely to work with one or two organizations until the number of subscriptions allows us to spread this partnership approach more widely.

Pause for thought ...

How is your present setting you up for the best chance of success in the future?

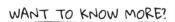

WANT TO KNOW MORE?

http://www.my31practices.com/the-book/resources/chapter-31

QUIZ

"Judge a man by his questions rather than by his answers."
Voltaire

In keeping with the interactive and action-oriented style of this book, have a go at this quick my31Practices quiz. The purpose is to help you understand the parts of the book that you have taken in and to identify areas you may wish to revisit. Some of the questions are light hearted, some easy, some more fundamental, and others more challenging. You can see the answers to the 31 questions when you turn over the next page:

1. What are "values"?

_____

2. Which character can my31Practices help you to release?

_____

3. How many parts are there in the book?

_____

4. How many hours of purposeful practice is the primary contributing factor (above natural talent) to excellence in sport and life?

_____

5. What is the best timing for positive reinforcement?

_____

6. What was the name of the programme used by Ritz Carlton and Marriott which inspired the creation of the 31Practices approach?

_____

7. Complete the missing word: The _____ treadmill.

_____

8. What are the four pillars of the 31Practices framework?

_____

9. How many myPractices do you need for each of your five myValues to get started?

_____

10. What are the three core elements of John Kabat-Zinn's definition of mindfulness?

_____

11. In which year did Alan create his first version of my31Practices?

_____

12. What are three of the six NLP Principles of Success?

_____

13. What does my31Practices help Lindsay's team of coaches to do?

_____

14. Finish this sentence: If it's possible for someone else, ...

_____

15. What are said to be our three brains?

   _____

16. Which sport does Muriël enjoy?

   _____

17. Who said: "Not everything that can be counted counts, and not everything that counts can be counted."?

   _____

18. According to Dan Pink, how many pictures is a metaphor worth?

   _____

19. How many pieces of information are we said to be able to process in any given moment?

   _____

20. With whom has Amanda found my31Practices to be of help outside of work?

   _____

21. What new word describes affirmations put into practice?

   _____

22. What three forms of alignment is NLP concerned with in relation to goals?

   _____

23. Who said: "Keep on, keepin' on." ?

   _____

24. What are the Vark learning preferences?

_____

25. What is the difference between a fact and a belief?

_____

26. Where does Lauren consider as one of the most beautiful places in the world?

_____

27. What additional element does the Hook Model have compared to the Habit Loop?

_____

28. What are the three main ways in which we filter our experience?

_____

29. What is the main focus with my31Practices: a) process goals or b) outcome goals?

_____

30. What is the name of the recently created survey which provides a stakeholder perception snapshot of the degree to which the organization is living the stated values?

_____

31. How many simple steps does my31Practices consist of?

_____

ANSWERS

1. Traits or qualities that represent deeply held beliefs (Chapter 6 *Values*).
2. Your VALUES Superhero (Chapter 4 *What*).
3. 6 (Chapter 1 *Guide*).
4. 10,000 (Chapter 12 *Practice*).
5. Immediately after an action (Chapter 13 *Reinforcement*).
6. Daily Basics (Chapter 30 *Beginning*).
7. Hedonic (Chapter 2 *Why*).
8. Identify, Action, Impact, Refine (Chapter 3 *How*).
9. One (Chapter 5 *Template*).
10. On purpose, in the present moment, non-judgmentally (Chapter 7 *Mindfulness*).
11. 2010 (Chapter 24 *Practitioner*).
12. Know your outcome, have excellent awareness, be flexible, operate from a physiology and psychology of excellence, build and maintain rapport, take action! (Chapter 15 *NLP*).
13. Coach (Chapter 23 *Coach*).
14. It is possible for you (Chapter 17 *Presuppositions*).
15. Head brain, heart brain, gut brain (Chapter 21 *mBIT*).
16. Softball (Chapter 25 *Traveller*).
17. William Bruce Cameron (Chapter 14 *Assessment*).
18. A thousand (Chapter 8 *Metaphor*).
19. Between five and nine (Chapter 18 *Awareness*).
20. Teenage children (Chapter 26 *Firestarter*).

21. Affirmactions (Chapter 9 *Affirmation*).
22. Actions and goals; actions and values; goals and environment (Chapter 19 *Alignment*).
23. Jacob Martin Engle (Chapter 27 *Changemaker*).
24. Visual, auditory, reading and writing, kinesthetic (Chapter 10 *Learning*).
25. A fact is irrefutable and a belief is a judgment/interpretation or assumption (Chapter 20 *Beliefs*).
26. Queensland, Australia (Chapter 28 *Seeker*).
27. User investment (Chapter 11 *Habit*).
28. Deletion, distortion, generalization (Chapter 16 *Maps*).
29. Process goals (Chapter 22 *Goals*).
30. corevaluescore survey (Chapter 31 *Present*).
31. Six (Chapter 29 *Recap*).

We would love to hear how many you answered correctly.

PAUSE FOR THOUGHT ...

Which parts of the book have "stuck" with you best – and why do you think this is?

ABOUT THE AUTHORS AND ILLUSTRATOR

ALAN WILLIAMS
Founder & MD, SERVICEBRAND GLOBAL

Alan coaches service-sector organizations, internationally and in the UK, to deliver inspiring service for competitive advantage. He is a published author and speaker whose projects have delivered measurable business results across a balanced scorecard and have been recognized with industry awards.

Alan thrives on leading the values-driven transformation of service, culture and behaviour and is an expert facilitator of experiential learning workshops. His first co-authored book, *The 31 Practices: Release the Power of Your Organization's VALUES... Every Day,* received international critical acclaim.

Alan is a board member of BQF, a founder faculty member of Culture University, a steering group member of the UK Values Alliance, and founder of the newly formed Global Values Alliance.

STEVE PAYNE
Founder & CEO of NLP Dynamics and
the Academy of Coaching and Training

Steve is an international executive coach, actor, writer and motivational speaker who has been helping individuals and organizations achieve their performance goals for over twenty years. As an actor Steve trained at the Central School of Speech and Drama in London and has worked in radio drama for BBC Radio 4, as well as appearing in theatre, film and television over many years. His television roles include appearances in some of the UK's best-known television series.

As a business coach, Steve has helped senior executives from blue chip companies to SMEs in Europe and South America achieve their full potential. He has developed training programmes that help companies deal with the challenges brought about by organizational change. Much of Steven's work in business is based on creating a values-based culture. Steven has also created coach-training programmes for the Academy of Coaching and Training (ACT), accredited by the Association for Coaching in the UK.

Steve is one of very few certified Master Trainers of Neuro Linguistic Programming in the world and has a passion for helping people overcome assumed limitations to reach their full potential. He runs certified training courses in Public Speaking, NLP and Coaching across Europe and South America.

JOHN MONTGOMERY

John is a conceptual artist, whiteboard animator, information product creator, entrepreneur, business consultant and business owner.

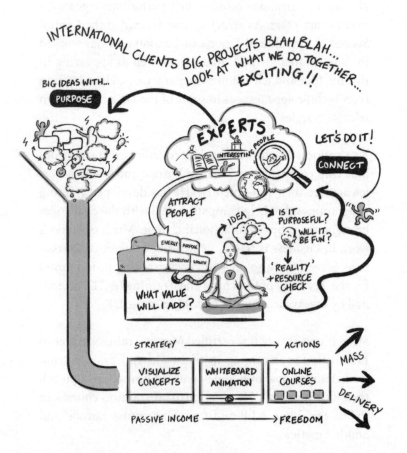

MYBIOG

Why not follow John's example and illustrate your own biography here:

WANT TO KNOW MORE?

http://www.my31practices.com/the-book/people/

ENDNOTES

Chapter 1 Guide

i.   *Harry Potter and the Chamber of Secrets*, by J K Rowling, published in 1998 is the second book in the series of seven Harry Potter books.

ii. Lindsay Myers, MBA, MPH, 23 May 2014, The Self-Help Industry Helps Itself to Billions of Dollars http://brainblogger.com/2014/05/23/the-self-help-industry-helps-itself-to-billions-of-dollars/ (accessed 10 January 2016).

iii. John D Hayes (born 1955) chief marketing officer, American Express.

iv. Alan Williams & Allison Whybrow *The 31Practices: Release the Power of Your Organization's VALUEs Every Day*, (London: LID Publishing, 2013)

v.   Lawrence Peter "Yogi" Berra (1925–2015) baseball player and coach http://www.yogi-berra.com/ (accessed 21 March 2016).

vi. http://www.theguardian.com/books/2013/dec/28/self-help-books-literature-publishers-growth (accessed 1 May 2016).

Chapter 2 Why

i.   Judy Garland (1922–1969) was an American singer, actress and vaudevillian.

ii.   http://www.nativevillage.org/Inspiration-/ten_native_american_commandments.htm (accessed 1 February 2016).

iii. Richard Layard, *Happiness: Lessons From a New Science*, (London: Penguin Books, 2005).

iv.   Ed Halliwell, *In the Face of Fear: How Fear and Anxiety Affect our Health and Society, and What We Can Do About It*, (Mental Health Foundation, 2009)

v.   *Work related Stress, Anxiety and Depression Statistics in Great Britain 2015*, (London: HSA Crown).

vi.   Opinium research poll (2009) commissioned by Mental Health Foundation referenced in http://www.livingmindfully.co.uk/downloads/Mindfulness_Report.pdf (accessed 1 February 2016).

vii. http://www.theglobeandmail.com/sports/chronology-of-the-tiger-woods-scandal/article4313560/?page=all (accessed 26 April 2016).

viii. Tiger Woods, ESPN interview, 21 March, 2010, http://www.notable-quotes.com/w/woods_tiger.html (accessed 1 February 2016).

ix.   Lucius Annaeus Seneca, *On the Shortness of Life*, translated by John W. Basore, Loeb Classical Library, (London: William Heinemann, 1932).

x.   Arnold Bennett (first published 1908), *How to Live on 24 Hours a Day*, (London: Hard Press, 2006).

xi.   Lucius Annaeus Seneca (c. 4 BC–AD 65) was a Roman Stoic philosopher, statesman, dramatist, and humorist of the Silver Age of Latin literature.

xii. Enoch Arnold Bennett (27 May 1867–27 March 1931) was an English writer.

xiii. Jon Kabbat-Zinn, *Coming to our Senses: Healing Ourselves and the World Through Mindfulness*, (London: New York: Piatkus , 2005).

xiv. David Robert Jones (1947–2016), known as David Bowie, was an English singer, songwriter, actor and record producer.

xv.   Muhammad Ali (born Cassius Marcellus Clay, Jr, 1942–2016) was an American professional boxer and civil rights champion.

xvi. Mihaly Csikszentmihalyi, *Flow: The Psychology of Happiness: The Classic Work on How to Achieve Happiness (1990)*.

xvii. E E Cummings (1894–1962) was an American poet, painter, essayist, author and playwright. Writing poems from the age of eight, he explored ideas such as purpose and inner strength, among many others.

xviii. Robert Dilts & Judith DeLozier, *The Encyclopedia of Systemic Neuro-Linguistic Programming and NLP New Coding*, (NLP University Press, 2000).

Chapter 3 What

i.   *The Tragedy of Hamlet, Prince of Denmark*, often shortened to Hamlet, is a tragedy written by William Shakespeare at an uncertain date between 1599 and 1602.

ii.   William Wordsworth (1770–1850) was an English Romantic poet.

iii. Alan Williams & Allison Whybrow, *The 31Practices: Release the Power of Your Organization's VALUES Every Day*, (London: LID Publishing, 2013).

iv.   W Edwards Deming, *Out of the Crisis: MIT Centre for Advanced Engineering, (1986)*.

v.   Walter A Shewhart, *Statistical Method from the Viewpoint of Quality Control*, (New York: Dover, 1939).

Chapter 4 How

i.   Pablo Ruiz y Picasso, also known as Pablo Picasso (1881–1973), was a Spanish painter, sculptor, printmaker, ceramicist, stage designer, poet and playwright.

ii.   Leonardo di ser Piero da Vinci, more commonly called Leonardo da Vinci, or Leonardo, (1452–1519), was an Italian polymath whose areas of interest included invention, painting, sculpting, architecture, science, music, mathematics, engineering, literature, anatomy, geology, astronomy, botany, writing, history, and cartography.

Chapter 5 Template

i. This idiom was included in *Parœmiologia Anglo-Latina*, a collection of proverbs in English and Latin that was published in London in 1639 by John Clarke (1596?–1658).

Chapter 6 Values

i. In fact, the original version is a calypso song written by jazz musicians Melvin "Sy" Oliver and James "Trummy" Young. It was first recorded in 1939 by Jimmie Lunceford, Harry James, and Ella Fitzgerald.

ii. Rosanna M Fiske: www.blogs.hbr.org/cs/2011/07/the_business_of_communicating.html by Rosanna M. Fiske (accessed 28 July 2013).

iii. Barrett Values Centre: Values Overview. http://www.valuescentre.com/values/?sec=values_overview (accessed 8 February 2013).

iv. Brian P Hall, *Values Shift: A Guide to Personal and Organizational Transformation*, (Twin Light Publishers, 1994).

v. Heidegger, M, *Being and Time*, translated by J Macquarie and E Robinson. (San Francisco: Harper, 1962).

vi. Dwight Lyman Moody (1837–1899), also known as D L Moody, was an American evangelist and publisher.

vii. Abraham Lincoln (1809–1865) was the 16th president of the United States.

Chapter 7 Mindfulness

i. Alan Alexander "A A" Milne (1882–1956) was an English author, best known for his books about the teddy bear Winnie-the-Pooh and for various poems.

ii. Oliver Kay, The Times, 23 March 2015, Key to Johanna Konta's breakthrough lies in living in the present. http://www.thetimes.co.uk/tto/sport/tennis/article4583906.ece?shareToken=267b6b17da2e4751b2216946df5a9ef3 (accessed 10 February 2016).

iii. David Rock & Linda Page, Coaching With the Brain in Mind: Foundations for Practice, (New Jersey: John Wiley & Sons, 2009).

iv. Daniel J Siegel, *The Mindful Brain: Reflection and Attunement in the Cultivation of Wellbeing*, (New York: Norton, 2007).

v. Tang YY, Ma Y, Wang J, Fan Y, Feng S, Lu Q, et al. (2007), "Short-term Meditation Training Improves Attention and Self-regulation", *Proceedings of the National Academy of Sciences of the United States of America*, 104. 17152-17156.

vi. Ellen Langer (January 13, 2016), "Mindfulness Isn't Much Harder than Mindlessness", Harvard Business Review

vii. David Rock and Linda Page, *Coaching with the Brain in Mind: Foundations for Practice*, (New Jersey: John Wiley & Sons, 2009).

viii. Richard J. Davidson (Author), Sharon Begley (Contributor) "The Emotional Life of Your Brain: How Its Unique Patterns Affect the Way You Think, Feel, and Live – and How You Can Change Them" (24 Dec 2012).

ix. http://www.wakehealth.edu/News-Releases/2015/Mindfulness_Meditation_Trumps_Placebo_in_Pain_Reduction.htm (accessed 1 May 2016).

x. George Bernard Shaw (1856 – 1950) was a playwright originally from Ireland. He wrote more than 50 plays over his lifetime, with the final play completed a few months before his death. Nobelprize.org. 18 Mar 2013 http://www.nobelprize.org/nobel_prizes/literature/laureates/1925/shaw-bio.html.

xi. Senge P, Jaworski J, Scharmer O, and Flowers S (2005), *Presence: Exploring Profound Change in People, Organizations and Society*, London: Nicholas Brealey.

xii. Staudinger, UM (2008). "A Psychology of Wisdom: History and Recent Developments", *Research in Human Development*, 5, 107-120.

xiii. William Aloysius Keane (1922–2011), better known as Bil Keane, was an American cartoonist.

xiv. Eckhart Tolle (born Ulrich Leonard Tölle 1948) is a German-born resident of Canada,[1][2] best known as the author of *The Power of Now* and *A New Earth: Awakening to Your Life's Purpose*.

xv. Thich Nhat Hanh, *Stepping into Freedom: Rules of Monastic Practice for Novices*. (Berkeley, CA: Parrallax Press, 1997).

xvi. Walter "Walt" Whitman 1819–1892) was an American poet, essayist and journalist.

xvii. Ellen Langer, (March 2014), "Mindfulness in the Age of Complexity", *Harvard Business Review*.

xviii. Marcus Aurelius (AD 26 April 121–17 March 180) was Roman Emperor from 161 to 180 whose stoic tome *Meditations*, written in Greek while on campaign between AD 170 and 180, is revered as a literary monument to a philosophy of service and duty.

xix. Tog-me Zong-po (1245–1369), *37 Practices of a Bodhisattva: A summary of how an awakening being behaves*. Tog-me the monk, a teacher of scripture and logic, composed this text in a cave near the town of Ngülchu Rinchen for his own and others' benefit. http://www.unfetteredmind.org/37-practices-of-a-bodhisattva (accessed 10 February 2016).

xx. Sharon Salzberg, *Real Happiness: The Power of Meditation*. (New York: Workman Publishing Co, 2011).

Chapter 8 Metaphor

i. Daniel H Pink, *A Whole New Mind: Why Right-Brainers Will Rule the Future*. (Marshall Cavendish, 2008).

ii. Rick Eigenbrod, Executive Coach and Organizational Development Consultant http://www.mydrivingseat.com/the-blog/week-24-tip-the-power-of-metaphors/and permission granted by email.

iii. Forrest Gump is a 1994 American epic romantic-comedy-drama film based on the 1986 novel of the same name by Winston Groom.

iv. Emily Elizabeth Dickinson (1830–1886) was an American poet.

v. Aristotle, *Poetics* (1459a).

vi. George Lakoff and Mark Johnson, *Metaphors We Live By*, (University of Chicago Press, 1980).

vii. Daniel H Pink, *A Whole New Mind: Moving from the Information Age to the Conceptual Age*, (New York: Riverhead Books, 2005).

viii. Ralph Waldo Emerson (1803–1882) was an American essayist, lecturer, and poet who led the Transcendentalist movement of the mid-19th century.

ix. William Shakespeare (1564–1616) was an English poet, playwright, and actor, widely regarded as the greatest writer in the English language and the world's pre-eminent dramatist.

x. Khalil Gibran, full Arabic name Gibran Khalil Gibran, (1883–1931) was a Lebanese-American artist, poet.

xi. Valentin Louis Georges Eugène Marcel Proust (1871–1922) was a French novelist, critic, and essayist.

xii. William Wordsworth (1770–1850) was a major English Romantic poet.

xiii. Elton John and Bernie Taupin (1973), *Candle in the Wind* – the song focuses on the life of Norma Jeane, AKA Marilyn Monroe, a world-famous actress from the 1950s. It chronicles her rise to fame and tragic death.

xiv. Jerry Leiber and Mike Stoller (1952), *Hound Dog* – recorded by Willie Mae "Big Mama" Thornton in 1952 and the best-known version is the recording by Elvis Presley (1956), his best-selling song (c10 million copies globally).

xv. Katy Perry, Mikkel S. Eriksen, Tor Erik Harnansen, Sandy Wilhelm, Ester Dean (2010) *Firework*.

Chapter 9 Affirmation

i. Muhammad Ali (born Cassius Marcellus Clay, Jr, 1942–2016) was an American professional boxer and civil rights champion.

ii. http://www.dictionary.com/browse/affirmation (accessed 15 January 2016).

iii. Émile Coué de la Châtaigneraie (1857–1926) was a French psychologist and pharmacist who introduced a popular method of psychotherapy and self-improvement based on optimistic autosuggestion.

iv. Michael J Losier, *Law of Attraction: The Science of Attracting More of What You Want and Less of What You Don't*, (New York: Grand Central Publishing, 2010).

v. Manprit Kaur, *The Little Book of Big Affirmations*, (India: 2014).

vi. Watty Piper, *The Little Engine That Could*; Illustrator: George and Doris Hauman, (US: Platt & Munk, 1930).

vii. The Empire Strikes Back (also known as *Star Wars: Episode V – The Empire Strikes Back*) is a 1980 American epic science fiction film directed by Irvin Kershner.

viii. Robin Sharma (born 1964) is a Canadian self-help writer.

ix. Emanuel James "Jim" Rohn (1930–2009) was an American entrepreneur, author and motivational speaker.

x. Epictetus (c. AD 55–135) was a Greek speaking Stoic philosopher.

Chapter 10 Learning

i. *All You Need Is Love* (1967) is a song by the Beatles, written by John Lennon and credited to Lennon–McCartney.

ii. Kendra Cherry (2016) *The Psychology of Learning* http://psychology.about.com/od/psychologystudyguides/a/learning_sg.htm (accessed 26 March 2016).

iii. Robert Burns, *The Adult Learner at Work*. (Sydney: Business and Professional Publishing, 1995).

iv. Melissa Hurst PhD (2013), *Behavioural, Cognitive, Developmental, Social Cognitive and Constructivist Perspectives* https://www.youtube.com/watch?v=Fdx2SYQRp7s (accessed 28 March 2016).

v. Coffield F, Moseley D, Hall E, Ecclestone K, *Learning styles and pedagogy in post-16 learning: a systematic and critical review*, (Learning & Skills Research Centre, 2004).

vi. (Great Britain) (LSRC).

vii. Pashler H, McDaniel M, Rohrer D, and Bjork R(2008), "Learning Styles: Concepts and Evidence", *Psychological Science in the Public Interest*, 9 (3) (accessed 28 March 2016).

viii. Dugan Laird, *Approaches to Training and Development*, (Reading, Mass.: Addison-Wesley, 1985).

ix. Chu S and Downes JJ (2002) Proust nose best: odors are better cues of autobiographical memory. Mem Cognit. 30 June 2002 (4):511-8. PubMed PMID: 12184552.

x. Benjamin Franklin (1706–1790) was one of the Founding Fathers of the United States. A renowned polymath, Franklin was a leading author, printer, political theorist, politician, freemason, postmaster, scientist, inventor, civic activist, statesman, and diplomat.

xi. Fleming, N D & Mills, C (1992), "Helping students understand how they learn", *The Teaching Professor*, 7 (4).

xii. Kenneth J Gergen & R Walter. (1998), "Real/izing the Relational," *Journal Of Social And Personal Relationships*, 15 (1), 110-126.

xiii. http://works.swarthmore.edu/fac-psychology/427 (accessed 29 March 2016).

xiv. McGill, I & Beaty, L, (1995), *Action Learning: A Guide for Professional, Managerial and Educational Development*.

xv. Confucius (551–479 BC) was a Chinese teacher, editor, politician, and philosopher of the Spring and Autumn period of Chinese history.

xvi. Henry Ford (1863–1947) was an American industrialist, the founder of the Ford Motor Company.

xvii. Robert Burns, *The Adult Learner at Work*, (Sydney: Business and Professional Publishing, 1995).

xviii. Leonardo di ser Piero da Vinci, more commonly Leonardo da Vinci or simply Leonardo (1452–1519), was an Italian polymath.

xix. Sir Richard Charles Nicholas Branson, (born 1950) is an English business magnate, investor, and philanthropist.

xx. Ian McGill & Liz Beaty, *Action Learning, Second edition: a guide for professional, management and educational development*, (London: Kogan Page, 1995).

xxi. Burns, S (1995), "Rapid changes require enhancement of adult learning", *HR Monthly* June, pp 16-17.

xxii. Carol S Dweck, *Mindset: The New Psychology of Success*, (Random House, 2006).

xxiii. B B King (born Riley B King) (1925–2015) was an American blues guitarist and singer. Widely considered one of the greatest and most respected blues guitarists of all time, and is possibly the most recognizable name in the blues genre.

Chapter II Habit

i. Will Durant, *The Story of Philosophy : The Lives and Opinions of the Greater Philosophers*, Simon and Schuster, (New York: Simon and Schuster, 1926).

ii. https://en.wikipedia.org/wiki/Habit (accessed 30 April 2016).

iii. Andrews, B R (1903), "Habit", *The American Journal of Psychology* (University of Illinois Press) 14 (2): 121–49.doi:10.2307/1412711. ISSN 0002-9556. JSTOR 1412711 – via JSTOR.

iv. Habituation, www.Animalbehaviouronline.com (retrieved 29 August, 2008).

v. Norman Rosenthal, *Habit Formation Sussex Directories*, Retrieved 30 November 2011.

vi. Habit Formation https://www.psychologytoday.com/basics/habit-formation (accessed 31 April 2016).

vii. André Maurois (born Émile Salomon Wilhelm Herzog) (1885–1967) was a French author.

viii. Nir Eyal (2014) Hooked: How to Build Habit-Forming Products, (Portfolio Penguin: New York, 2014).

ix. Charles Duhigg (2014) *The Power of Habit: Why We Do What We Do in Life and Business*, (Penguin Random House: New York, 2014).

x. Norton M, Mochon D, Ariely D, Copyright © 2011 The "IKEA Effect": When Labor Leads to Love Working Paper, HBS http://www.hbs.edu/faculty/Publication%20Files/11-091.pdf (accessed 23 February 2016).

xi. http://blogs.discovermagazine.com/neuroskeptic/2012/05/09/the-70000-thoughts-per-day-myth/#.VyzOBIQrLIV (accessed 20 April 2016).

xii. Daniel Kahneman (born 1934) is an Israeli-American psychologist notable for his work on the psychology of judgment and decision-making, as well as behavioural economics.

xiii. Deepak Chopra (born 1947) is an Indian American author, public speaker, alternative medicine advocate, and a prominent figure in the New Age movement.

xiv. Richard H Thaler & Cass R Sunstein, *Nudge: Improving Decisions About Health, Wealth and Happiness*, (New Haven CT, Yale University Press, 2008).

xv. Gary Klein, *Sources of Power: How People Make Decisions*, (MIT Press, 1999).

xvi. Hermann Karl Hesse (1877–1962) was a German-born Swiss poet, novelist, and painter.

xvii. Dean Karlan, Margaret Mcconnell, Sendhil Mullainathan, Jonathan Zinman, *Getting to the Top of Mind: How Reminders Increase Saving* (NBER Working Paper No. 16205), Cambridge, MA: National Bureau of Economic Research, 2010).

xviii. http://blog.trello.com/the-psychology-of-checklists-why-setting-small-goals-motivates-us-to-accomplish-bigger-things/ (accessed 20 April 2016).

xix. Aristotle (384-322 BC) was a Greek philosopher and scientist.

xx. http://www.fastcompany.com/3022830/how-to-be-a-success-at-everything/the-secret-to-changing-your-habits-start-incredibly-small (accessed 30 April 2016).

Chapter 12 Practice

i. Fay Weldon (born 1931) is an English author, essayist and playwright.

ii. Mahatma Gandhi (1869–1948), born in Gujarat. The leader of the Indian Nationalist movement against British rule and widely considered the father of his country. His doctrine of non-violent protest has been hugely influential.

iii. Practise, as defined by the Oxford Dictionary Online. http://oxforddictionaries.com/definition/english/practice (accessed on 27 January 2013).

iv. Martha Graham, American dancer, teacher and choreographer of modern dance (1894–1991).

v. Kirk Mango, *Becoming a true champion: Achieving athletic excellence from the inside out*, (Maryland: Rowman & Littlefield, 2012).

vi. Charles McGrath (1997), "Elders on Ice", *The New York Times Magazine*, http://www.nytimes.com/1997/03/23/magazine/elders-on-ice.html?pagewanted=all&src=pm (accessed 1 August 2013).

vii. Gary Player, nicknamed the "black knight", is regarded as one of the great players in the history of golf.

viii. Malcolm Gladwell, *Blink: The Power of Thinking Without Thinking.* (London: Penguin, 2005).

ix. Matthew Syed, *Bounce: The Myth of Talent and the Power of Practice* (New York: Harper Perennial, 2011).

x. Malcolm Gladwell (2011). *Outliers: The Story of Success*, (London: Penguin, 2011).

xi. Donald Schon, *The Reflective Practitioner,* (Aldershot: Ashgate Publishing Ltd, 1991).

xii. Eric Lindros (born1973) is a Canadian professional ice hockey player.

xiii. Charles Edward "Ed" Macauley (1928–2011) was a professional basketball player in the NBA.

xiv. This curve is a combination of Elizabeth Kubler-Ross's cycle of grief which is commonly referred to as the change cycle and the competence cycle described by W. Lewis Robinson, which builds on others work and ancient traditions. See W. Lewis Robinson (1974), "Conscious Competency – The Mark of a Competent Instructor", *The Personnel Journal*, Baltimore, Volume 53, PP538-539; and Kubler-Ross, E (1973), *On Death and Dying*, London: Routledge.

xv. Jim Gillette, "Stages of competence" http://www.personal-growth-and-freedom.com/competence.html (accessed 18 April 2013).

xvi. Publilius Syrus, 1st century B C. A Syrian, brought as a slave to Italy, but through his wit and talent won the favour of his master who freed and educated him.

xvii. https://www.psychologytoday.com/blog/prefrontal-nudity/201208/smile-powerful-tool (accessed 24 April 2016).

Chapter 13 Reinforcement

i. Mary Kay Ash (1918–2001) was an American businesswoman and founder of cosmetics firm Mary Kay Inc, who was known for "praising people to success".

ii. Ivan Pavlov, *The Work of the Digestive Glands*, (London, Griffin, 1897/1902).

iii. Burrhus Skinner, *Science and human behaviour*. SimonandSchuster.com.

iv. David M Buss & Nancy Cantor (1989). European Journal of Personality

v. Personality Judith Haracksiewicz, "Chapter 8 Performance Evaluation and Intrinsic Motivation Processes: The Effects of Achievement Orientation and Rewards", *Personality psychology: Recent trends and emerging directions* (New York and Berlin, 1989).

vi.   Charles Duhigg, *The Power of Habit: Why We Do What We Do, and How to Change*, (New York: Random House, 2013).

vii. http://www.actionforhappiness.org/take-action/find-three-good-things-each-day (accessed 10 January 2016).

viii. Michael Armstrong, *Employee Reward Management And Practice*. Bell & Bain, (Great Britain: Bell & Bain, 2007).

ix.   Robert B. Dilts, *Visionary leadership skills: Creating a World to Which People Want to Belong*, (Meta Publications, 1996).

x.   https://www.psychologytoday.com/blog/the-athletes-way/201603/neurofeedback-

Chapter 14 Assessment

i.   Fernando Flores (born 1943) was the Chilean finance minister who spent three years as a political prisoner before being forced into exile to the US, where he developed his work on philosophy, coaching and workflow technology.

ii.   Grand Theft Auto is an open world action-adventure video game developed by DMA Design and published by BMG Interactive.

iii. http://www.ccsinsight.com/press/company-news/1944-smartwatches-and-smart-bands-dominate-fast-growing-wearables-market (accessed 24 April 2016).

iv.   Richard O Mason, & E Burton Swanson, *Measurements for Management Decision*. (Reading, MA: Addison-Wesley, 1981).

v.   Thomas Spencer Monson (born 21 August1927) is an American religious leader and author.

vi.   James Harrington, H, PhD, (born: January 16, 1929) is an author, international performance improvement guru and businessman. He developed many concepts, some of the more important ones include: Poor-Quality Cost, Total Improvement Management and Business Process Improvement.

vii. Latham & Locke (1981), "Goal Setting and Task Performance: 1969–1980" *Psychological Bulletin*, 90 (I), 125-152, American Psychological Association, Inc.

viii. A Boros, *Measurement Evaluation, English Translation Gabor, (Amsterdam: Elsevier, 1989)*.

ix.   R L Miller, P Brickman & D Bolen (1975), "Attribution v's Persuasion as a Means For Modifying Behaviour," *Journal of Personality and Social Psychology*: 3: 430-441.

x.   Kendra Cherry (2016), "Differences Between Extrinsic and Intrinsic Motivation?" https://www.verywell.com/differences-between-extrinsic-and-intrinsic-motivation-2795384 (accessed 28 April 2016).

xi.   David G Myers, *Psychology, Eighth Edition in Modules*, (Worth Publishers, 2007).

xii. Cameron (1963), "Informal Sociology: A Casual Introduction to Sociological Thinking". Often mistakenly attributed to Einstein.illuminates-personalized-ways-self-motivate (accessed 26 April 2016).

Chapter 15 NLP

i. This quote is attributed to many people, including Chinese philosopher Lao Tzu.

ii. Science Digest magazine.

iii. Joseph O'Connor, John Seymour, *Introducing NLP*, (Mandala, 1990).

iv. John Grinder & Frank Pucelik, *The Origins of Neuro Linguistic Programming*, (Crown House Publishing, 2013).

v. John Grinder & Carmen Bostic St. Clair, *Whispering in the Wind*, (J & C Enterprises, 2001).

vi. Andrew Z. Cohen, *Shining Light on Your Unconscious Values*, (Huffington Post, 2011).

vii. Nike is an American multinational corporation that is engaged in the design, development, manufacturing and worldwide marketing and sales of footwear, apparel, equipment, accessories and services.

viii. Fritz Perls, (1893–1970) the father of Gestalt Therapy.

ix. Robert Dilts & Judith DeLozier, The Encyclopedia of Systemic Neuro-Linguistic Programming and NLP New Coding (NLP University Press, 2000).

x. NLP Presupposition. See the ANLP website: http://www.anlp.org/presuppositions-of-nlp

xi. The National Institute for Health: https://www.nlm.nih.gov/medlineplus/magazine/issues/winter08/articles/winter08pg4.html

xii. Ornish D, et al. (1983), "Effects of Stress Management Training and Dietary Changes in Treating Ischemic Heart Disease", *JAMA*, 249: 54–59.

xiii. https://www.heartmath.org (accessed 30 April 2016).

xiv. Elbert Green Hubbard (1856–1915) was an American writer, publisher, artist, and philosopher.

xv. Happiness Manifesto http://gretchenrubin.com/happiness_project/2009/02/check-out-my-happiness-manifesto-brand-new/ (accessed 30 April 2016).

xvi. This quote is attributed to Albert Einstein, but there does not seem to be documentary evidence that this quote actually came from Einstein.

xvii. Colin Luther Powell (born 1937) is an American statesman and a retired four-star general in the United States Army.

xviii. Tony D'Angelo (born 1972) is an American educational entrepreneur.

xix. Thomas Jefferson (1743–1826) was an American Founding Father who was principal author of the Declaration of Independence.

Chapter 16 Maps

i. Wayne Dyer (1940–2015) was an internationally renowned author and speaker in the field of self-development.

ii.   Karl Marx (1818–1883) was a philosopher, economist, sociologist, journalist, and revolutionary socialist.

iii.   Robert Dilts & Judith DeLozier, The Encyclopedia of Systemic Neuro-Linguistic Programming and NLP New Coding (NLP University Press, 2000).

iv.   Dilts R & DeLozier J (2000). The Encyclopedia of Systemic Neuro-Linguistic Programming and NLP New Coding. NLP University Press.

v.   John Grinder & Carmen Bostic St. Clair, *Whispering in the Wind*, (J & C Enterprises, 2001).

vi.   Robert Dilts & Judith DeLozier, The Encyclopedia of Systemic Neuro-Linguistic Programming and NLP New Coding (NLP University Press, 2000).

vii.   http://www.ascd.org/ASCD/pdf/journals/ed_lead/el200912_willis.pdf (accessed 30 May 2016)

viii. Webb C (2016), *How to Have a Good Day*, Crown Business.

ix.   Daniel J Simons & Daniel T Levin (1998), "Failure to detect changes to people during a real-world interaction", *Psychonomic Bulletin & Review*, 5 (4): 644–649.

Chapter 17 Presuppositions

i.   Randy Pausch, Professor of Computer Science, Human-Computer Interaction, and Design at Carnegie Mellon University, Pittsburgh, Pennsylvania. Pausch said these words in his famous Last Lecture in 2007.

ii.   Robert Dilts & Judith DeLozier, The Encyclopedia of Systemic Neuro-Linguistic Programming and NLP New Coding (NLP University Press, 2000).

iii.   Stefan Klein, *The Science of Happiness*, (Marlowe & Company, 2006).

iv.   Ken Blanchard, *Self-Leadership and the 1-Minute Manager – Discover the Magic of No Excuses*, (Harper Collins, 2006).

v.   This quote has often been associated with Anthony Robbins, Albert Einstein, Henry Ford, and others.

vi.   George Bernard Shaw (1856–1950), known at his insistence simply as Bernard Shaw, was an Irish playwright, critic and polemicist.

vii.   Constantin Stanislavski (1863–1938) was a Russian actor, theatre director and creator of methods for training actors.

viii. Constantin Stanislavski (1936). *An Actor Prepares*, (Theatre Arts, 1936).

ix.   Ornish ,D et al. (1983), "Effects of stress management training and dietary changes in treating ischemic heart disease", *JAMA*, 249: 54–59.

x.   Sathya Sai Baba (born Sathya Narayana Raju (1926–2011) was an Indian guru, and philanthropist.

xi.   Harsha Bhogle (born 1961) is an Indian cricket commentator and journalist.

xii.   Frank Herbert, American writer, journalist, ecological consultant and lecturer (1920–1986).

xiii. Miley Ray Cyrus (born Destiny Hope Cyrus, 1992) is an American singer, songwriter, and actress.

xiv. Plato (428/427 or 424/423–348/347 BC) was a philosopher in Classical Greece.

xv. George Bernard Shaw (1856–1950) was an Irish playwright, critic and polemicist.

xvi. Audre Lorde (born Audrey Geraldine Lorde) (1934–1992) was a Caribbean-American writer, radical feminist, womanist, lesbian, and civil rights activist.

Chapter 18 Awareness

i. Stephen R. Covey (2004) The 7 Habits of Highly Effective People: Powerful Lessons in Personal Change, (London: Simon & Schuster UK Ltd, 2004).

ii. http://www.nlpdynamics.com/2016/05/12/8586/ (accessed 19 May 2016).

iii. Eckhart Tolle (born 1948) is the author of *The Power of Now* and *A New Earth: Awakening to your Life's Purpose.*

iv. Robert Dilts & Judith DeLozier, The Encyclopedia of Systemic Neuro-Linguistic Programming and NLP New Coding (NLP University Press, 2000).

v. Robert Dilts & Judith DeLozier, The Encyclopedia of Systemic Neuro-Linguistic Programming and NLP New Coding (NLP University Press, 2000).

vi. George A. Miller (1956), "The Magical Number Seven, Plus or Minus Two: Some Limits on Our Capacity for Processing Information", *The Psychological Review*, 63, pp. 81-97.

vii. Wayne Walter Dyer (1940–2015) was an American philosopher, self-help author, and a motivational speaker.

viii. John Grinder & Carmen Bostic St Clair C, *Whispering in the Wind*, (J & C Enterprises, 2001).

ix. Mehrabian, A., and Ferris, S.R. (1967), Inference of Attitudes from Nonverbal Communication in Two Channels", *Journal of Consulting Psychology*. 31 (3): 1967, 248–252. - not as currently in the endnotes (Note: please match font with rest of copy).

Chapter 19 Alignment

i. Brian Tracy (born 1944) is an American motivational speaker and author.

ii. Robert Dilts & Judith DeLozier, The Encyclopedia of Systemic Neuro-Linguistic Programming and NLP New Coding (NLP University Press, 2000).

iii. http://www.nlpdynamics.com/2016/05/09/occupational-stress-can-nlp-help/ (accessed 19 May 2016).

iv. http://www.hse.gov.uk/statistics/dayslost.htm (accessed 1 May 2016).

v. http://www.nlpdynamics.com/2016/05/09/occupational-stress-can-nlp-help/ (accessed 1 May 2016).

vi. James M Kouzes & Barry Z Posner, *The Truth About Leadership: The No-fads, Heart-of-the matter Facts You Need to Know*, (San Francisco, CA: Jossey-Bass , 2010).

Chapter 20 Beliefs

i. Tony Robbins (born 1960) is an American entrepreneur and best-selling author.

ii. Robert Dilts & Judith DeLozier, The Encyclopedia of Systemic Neuro-Linguistic Programming and NLP New Coding (NLP University Press, 2000).

iii. Thomas Paine (1737–1809) was an English-American political activist, philosopher, political theorist, and revolutionary.

iv. Norman Doidge, The Brain That Changes Itself, (Penguin Books, 2015). Doidge is a distinguished scientist, a medical doctor, a psychiatrist on the faculty of both the University of Toronto and of Columbia University in New York.

v. Norman Doidge is a distinguished scientist, a medical doctor, a psychiatrist on the faculty of both the University of Toronto and of Columbia University in New York.

vi. https://www.theguardian.com/science/2015/feb/08/norman-doidge-brain-healing-neuroplasticity-interview (accessed 17 May 2016).

vii. William James (1842–1910) was an American philosopher and psychologist.

viii. William Somerset Maugham CH (1874–1965) was a British playwright, novelist and short-story writer.

ix. Dr Debasish Mridha is an American physician, philosopher, poet seer, and author.

x. Nineteen Eighty-Four, often published as 1984, is a dystopian novel by English author George Orwell published in 1949.

xi. Richard Bandler & John Grinder, The Structure of Magic I, (Science and Behaviour Books, 1975).

xii. Richard Bandler & John Grinder, The Structure of Magic I, (Science and Behaviour Books, 1975).

xiii. With thanks to Jeremy Lazarus (NLP Master Trainer) for this structure.

xiv. John Grinder & Richard Bandler, Patterns of the Hypnotic Techniques of Milton H Erickson: Volumes 1 & 2 (Meta Publications, 1975).

xv. Milton H Erickson (1901–1980) was an American psychiatrist and psychologist specializing in hypnosis and family therapy.

Chapter 21 mBIT

i. Cara Fiorina (born 1954) is an American businesswoman and political candidate.

ii. Grant Soosalu & Marvin Oka, mBraining: Using Your Multiple Brains to Do Cool Things (CreativeSpace Independent Publishing Platform, 2012).

iii. Grant Soosalu & Marvin Oka, mBraining: Using Your Multiple Brains to Do Cool Things (CreativeSpace Independent Publishing Platform, 2012).

Chapter 21 mBIT

i. Cara Fiorina (born 1954) is an American businesswoman and political candidate.

ii. Grant Soosalu & Marvin Oka, *mBraining: Using Your Multiple Brains to Do Cool Things* (CreativeSpace Independent Publishing Platform, 2012).

iii. Grant Soosalu & Marvin Oka, *mBraining: Using Your Multiple Brains to Do Cool Things* (CreativeSpace Independent Publishing Platform, 2012).

iv. Deepak Chopra is an Indian American author, public speaker, alternative medicine advocate, and a prominent figure in the New Age movement.

v. Grant Soosalu & Marvin Oka, *mBraining: Using Your Multiple Brains to Do Cool Things* (CreativeSpace Independent Publishing Platform, 2012).

vi. Davidson R J, Kabat-Zinn J, Schumacher J, Rosenkranz M, Muller D, Santorelli SF, Urbanowski F, Harrington A, Bonus K, Sheridan JF, "Alterations in brain and immune function produced by mindfulness meditation", *Psychosom Med.* Jul–Aug; 65(4): 564–70.

vii. Grant Soosalu & Marvin Oka, *mBraining: Using Your Multiple Brains to Do Cool Things* (CreativeSpace Independent Publishing Platform, 2012).

viii. Doc L Childre, Howard Martin & Donna Beech, *The HeartMath Solution: The Institute of HeartMath's Revolutionary Program for Engaging the Power of the Heart's Intelligence* (HarperOne, 2000).

ix. Mayer E (2011), "Gut feelings: the emerging biology of gut–brain communication", *Nature Reviews Neuroscience*, 12: 453–466.

x. Grant Soosalu & Marvin Oka, *mBraining: Using Your Multiple Brains to Do Cool Things* (CreativeSpace Independent Publishing Platform, 2012).

Chapter 22 Goals

i. Hilary Hinton "Zig" Ziglar (1926–2012) was an American author, salesman, and motivational speaker.

ii. Joseph O'Connor & Andrea Lages, *Coaching with NLP* (Element/Harper Collins, 2004).

iii. Simon Sinek, *Start With Why,* (Penguin, 2011).

iv. https://www.psychologytoday.com/blog/wired-success/201104/why-goal-setting-doesnt-work (accessed 1 May 2016).

v. http://www.theguardian.com/lifeandstyle/2014/nov/07/systems-better-than--goals-oliver-burkeman (accessed 1 May 2016).

vi. Pablo Picasso was a Spanish painter, sculptor, printmaker, ceramicist, stage designer, poet and playwright who spent most of his adult life in France.

vii. Locke, EA and Latham, GP (2002), "Building a practical useful theory of goalsetting and task motivation: a 35 year odyssey", *American psychologist*, 57 (9), 705–717.

viii. An MOT (Ministry of Transport) test is an annual test of vehicle safety and roadworthiness in the UK (Road Traffic Act 1988)

ix. Deci EL, Ryan RM (2000), "The 'What' and 'Why' of Goal Setting, Human Needs and the Self-Determination of Behaviour", *Psychological Enquiry,* 11(4), 227–268.

x. Esther & Jerry Hicks, *Ask and It Is Given: Learning to Manifest Your Desires* (Hay House, 2004).

xi. Albert Einstein (1879–1955) was a Nobel Prize-winning physicist who published the special and general theories of relativity.

Chapter 23 Coach

i. Joel A Barker (born 1955) is an American futurist, author, lecturer and film maker.

Chapter 24 Practitioner

i. Vincent Willem van Gogh (1853–1890) was a Dutch post-Impressionist painter who said: "Great things are done by a series of small things brought together."

ii. Nelson Rolihlahla Mandela (1918–2013) was a South African anti-apartheid revolutionary, politician, and philanthropist, who served as president of South Africa from 1994–1999. He said: "It always seems impossible until it's done."

Chapter 26 Firestarter

i. Mohandas Karamchand Gandhi (1869–1948) was the pre-eminent leader of the Indian independence movement in British-ruled India.

Chapter 29 Recap

i. Laozi (also Lao Tzu or Lao-Tze) was an ancient Chinese philosopher, writer and the founder of philosophical Taoism.

ii. John Robert Wooden (1910–2010) was an American basketball player and coach.

iii. Benjamin Franklin (1706–1790) was one of the Founding Fathers of the United States. A renowned polymath, Franklin was a leading author, printer, political theorist, politician, freemason, postmaster, scientist, inventor, civic activist, statesman, and diplomat.

iv. Roy Edward Disney, KCSG (1930–2009) was a long-serving senior executive for The Walt Disney Company, which his father Roy Oliver Disney and his uncle Walt Disney founded.

Chapter 30 Beginning

i. Anton Pavlovich Chekhov (1860–1904) was a Russian playwright and short-story writer.

ii. Confucius (551–479 BC) was a Chinese teacher, editor, politician, and philosopher of the Spring and Autumn Period of Chinese history. The philosophy of Confucius emphasized personal and governmental morality, correctness of social relationships, justice and sincerity.

iii. Lois McMaster Bujold (born 1949) is an American speculative fiction writer.

iv. Emery Allen is an American writer and poet.

v. Kenneth Campbell "Ken" Stott (born 1954) is a Scottish stage, television and film actor.

vi. José Manuel Durão Barroso (born 1956) is a Portuguese politician who was the 11th President of the European Commission.

vii. Ken Poirot is an American businessman and author.

Chapter 31 Present

i. Mohandas Karamchand Gandhi (1869–1948) was the pre-eminent leader of the Indian independence movement in British-ruled India.

ii. Thích Nhất Hạnh (born as Nguyen Xuan Bao 1926) is a Vietnamese Buddhist monk, teacher, author, poet and peace activist.

iii. Lucius Annaeus Seneca, often known as Seneca the Younger or simply Seneca, (4 BC–AD 65) was a Roman Stoic philosopher, statesman and dramatist.

iv. James M Kouzes & Barry Z Posner, *The Leadership Challenge (New York: Wiley, 2007).*

WANT TO KNOW MORE?

http://www.my31practices.com/the-book/resources/